Uninvited Guest

Jenny Robertson writes books for adults and children. Her poems and children's stories have been read on Scottish Television, and a play by her was performed in the Edinburgh Festival Fringe. She has published three collections of poems, one of which was read in the 1989 Edinburgh Book Festival. She has edited a poetry anthology. She and her husband Stuart are currently working in St Petersburg, where Jenny is co-authoring in Russian a handbook on the Bible using creative work produced by children she has taught.

Uninvited Guest

A family's journey in schizophrenia

JENNY ROBERTSON

the christian
fellowship
of healing
(scotland)

6 Morningside Road,
EDINBURGH EH10 4DD
Tel: 0131 228 6553

TRIANGLE

First published in Great Britain in 1997
Triangle
SPCK
Holy Trinity Church
Marylebone Road
London NW1 4DU

British Library Cataloguing in Publication Data

A catalogue record of this book is available from
the British Library

ISBN 0–281–05096–1

Typeset by Pioneer Associates, Perthshire
Printed in Great Britain by
Caledonian International, Glasgow

Contents

CHAPTER 1

The Blessing of Sorrow

———————

Tourism can be a money-spinner. A holiday snapshot never tells the whole story to friends and family at home, so we buy souvenirs. Yet the things which tempt us abroad are usually too ethnic, too exotic, too heavy, too flimsy – or simply look out of place once we get home. Nevertheless, we keep on travelling, whether it be to Blackpool or Bombay, and we keep bringing back mementoes – we want our friends to share our holiday experiences, too.

So, here I am, opening the family album. There won't be any pictures of the 'me and the Taj Mahal' variety, although my journey includes physical travel. The real voyage has turned out to be an inner pilgrimage that is very different from anything I could have imagined, through a landscape which is often rough, even perilous. Signposts along the way often appear to be written in a language I haven't learnt to read yet or they point out terrain where I fear to tread.

My souvenir, too, was one I never expected to acquire. I had no idea what to do with it when I unpacked it. I still don't know for sure if I like it. It has been described to me as a blessing – the blessing of sorrow.

Here's the first photograph. The city I'm in is still called Leningrad. It will soon revert to its original name, St Petersburg, but this is 1989. The first cracks are appearing in the all but impenetrable wall which cut Russia off from the wider world for 72 years.

1

My husband, Stuart, and I have been involved with the former USSR in various ways for many years. Now, testing the new 'openness' which was proclaimed by the President, Gorbachev, after the leak of nuclear power at Chernobyl, we're staying privately as the guests of Russian friends – the first time such a thing has been possible since the doors closed in the 1920s.

At home we have left our son and daughter. Elaine is almost 19. She's tall like her father and, also like him, she has a great love of languages. She spent a year in Seville when she was only 17, perfecting her Spanish. When she returned, she got an unconditional acceptance onto her chosen course at college in Edinburgh in 1988, but things are going very wrong in her life, puzzlingly so. She is unhappy and she can't explain why. The world is becoming a dark and unpleasant place, but she is a strong person and extremely intelligent so she masks her inner turmoil, except that sometimes it breaks out in frenzied weeping which she can never explain.

Here, in her own words, is a description of what was going on in her mind at that time. It's an acutely perceived view, sharper than any photograph, of a young person whose world is falling apart. Elaine wrote this in March 1990, a year after our visit to Leningrad, but she didn't show it to me in full until I was writing this book. 'I feel so happy about that. It makes me feel better about myself', she said, and offered me her personal analysis. Here's how it begins.

Here are some brief comments jotted down in an attempt to communicate the way I feel. As I write it down, I feel that nobody can pass an opinion, stare blankly at me, dish out some useless advice or recite some useless fact at me.

There is a big wall between me and everyone that

I've put up to protect my dignity. I feel that even being in the company of certain people is a mockery to my whole being. I feel that there is scorn and condescension in everyone's voice and in the manner in which they speak to me. People now have the ability to make me look small and insignificant. I feel totally powerless to overcome this feeling as I also know that it is due to my paranoia and that I have probably brought it on myself. This in itself makes me feel incredibly vulnerable. I feel terribly foolish in the company of most people. I feel that people can detect my shame and my disgrace. I find myself avoiding eye contact – the hurt must be very blatantly written across my face and in my eyes. This I know, because I put it there and made no attempt to hide it for a long time. I thought people would see it and immediately understand and be more careful. How foolish I was!

Because of my pride, and because I had simply never needed to do it before, I did not seek someone wise whom I trusted to tell all to and then lay it to rest. I naively trusted everyone, just as I'd always done. I seemed incapable of adjusting, getting into gear. I was probably suffering from culture shock for quite some time after returning from Spain. I sought undemanding companionship, forgetting that every relationship has to be worked at and requires some effort. I also did not realize that people change in a year and so had I, quite drastically. I had lost a good deal of my dignity and also some control over my life. I was less confident. I had been so looking forward to coming home and to everything being the way it was before, and nothing was.

People have taken advantage of my silence, my depression, my inattentiveness, my mental exhaustion. People also took advantage of my lack of confidence, my desperate need to be heard (because I always had been heard before and now it was taking twice the effort). They used this to talk down to me, to treat me like some mental retard (so it seemed at the worst moments), to relate to me as somebody with an IQ minus and the mentality of a three-year-old. There no longer remains one single person who respects my right to speak. I have been so introspective and have brooded to myself rather than participating. I'm screaming inside at people and what they have reduced me to. I withdraw further and further all the time. I have no defences and feel totally and utterly vulnerable. My pride won't allow the fact to sink in that all this has really happened to me, so I retreat further.

Her father and I had no idea that Elaine felt like this – all we knew was that she was becoming very hard to live with. Elaine was our second child. We welcomed the pregnancy and her birth was completely normal. We had no idea that the uninvited guest – the title of this book – was lurking in the shadows when our little princess, our Briar Rose, was born that cold August morning on the Feast of St Clare in 1970.

The Uninvited Guest

Long and slender, my baby swam
on breaking waves to birth.

Kindly voices asked her name –
ward maid, doctor, nurse.

No one saw the dark shadow come,
the uninvited guest.

No one guessed the danger,
or undid the curse.

4

'No, they didn't, did they?' Elaine commented when she read this poem recently.

For now, however, let's stay with the pages of the Russian album dated 1989. It's the middle of April and the snow is beginning to melt in Leningrad. A bitter wind blows icily among the broad boulevards bordered by horrendous jerry-built tower blocks.

Our arrival has caused our hosts some trouble. Food can be a problem in Russia, where people are tremendously hospitable. We have arrived in the middle of Lent, and in Russia this is traditionally an eight-week fast. Our friends are trying to observe the dietary requirements of Russian Orthodoxy: on the first week of Lent you miss out meat, the next Sunday fish is omitted, then comes pancake week and, after that, eggs and all dairy products are taken off the menu until Easter. In this society, 'fast food' means food which is permitted during a period of abstinence, and has nothing to do with the Western-style burger or the deep-frozen, prepacked meal, totally unknown in Russia as yet. However, in the vast majority of Leningrad's homes in 1989, the cuisine isn't influenced by the age-old traditions of Lent because all forms of religion have been suppressed for 70 years.

Long queues form outside State vodka shops. We pass one every time we go to the tram stop. Stuart takes a photo. We put me in the foreground so that no one in the queue would think that they're being made the focus of a Westerner's camera. So my first snapshot *is* a 'me and . . .' one after all – 'me and the vodka queue'.

The light which shines across melted puddles of ice is very strong and bright. Spring is definitely on the way and there is a also an exhilarating freeing-up of thought. Stuart is involved in long, intellectual discussions seated on hard stools around kitchen tables. He is meeting the Leningrad underground – people, not trains! Here are some of the top brains of the city, men in their thirties and forties who work as janitors and night watchmen or stoke the fires which keep the essential central heating systems going. Discussion which ranges from poetry to philosophy, the liturgy and art, includes animated debate on the best types of fuel to use to achieve a good heat.

We've been involved in this kind of discussion before, or, rather, Stuart has – my Russian was still too limited. We have been travelling to the USSR on package tours for the last five years, taking clothing, necessities, what books we can, and, above all, that forbidden commerce: talk. We met the families of Christian prisoners and their friends, mainly among the Orthodox of Moscow and Leningrad. One of these men came up with a nickname for us, and others like us: travellers who went out heavily laden and returned with empty suitcases, though with minds and hearts full of impressions which no travel agency could ever supply. 'Tell us about the Soviet Union,' I asked him once. 'What is there to say? This is the Land of Mordor,' he replied, 'and you are hobbits.' Our friend was referring to Tolkien's saga, *Lord of the Rings*, which was widely read in Russia, though no official bookseller stocked it.

It was an apt description. Tolkien's Land of Mordor was the land of shadows which was watched over by one all-seeing eye – just as a totalitarian system closely controls the everyday life of its people, and of visitors. The network of control extended far beyond the tedious search through visitors' luggage at Customs. It certainly included the floor lady in the hotel whose duty was to sit at a table on 24-hour-long shifts and give out keys. It's said that if tourists were picked up at Customs, the smiling tour guide would pass the word to the floor lady who would switch on the bugging device in their rooms. This may simply be a piece of folklore because closed political systems fuel rumour. Certainly it happened more than once that if Stuart or I were picked up at Customs in Moscow for having a book by a forbidden author, which included a Bible, even though each tourist was officially allowed one copy, we would be singled out for an extra-thorough search on the way out in Leningrad.

I haven't any photographs – it would have been awkward, to say the least, to stand in the Customs hall and take a picture of my husband in his heavy winter coat opening his suitcase in front of Customs officials, but we'll imagine some.

It's 1984, my first ever visit to Russia. I got through Customs without incident, but Stuart excited their suspicions – just like a Levi's advert later, he had three pairs of unworn jeans in his case. Not only that, he had hardly any cash! In addition, he had books the Customs officials didn't like. So, they nabbed him. My photograph would show my husband's feet, all I could see of him as I bent down on the other side of the darkened glass which separated the Customs hall from the general public. Darkened it may have been, but it didn't quite reach the ground and, if I bent down, I could see his boots, trouser legs and coat hem as he was marched to and fro between two other pairs of feet. I remember thinking, 'If he gets chucked out of here, how am I going to manage on my own, knowing no Russian?'

Another might show him opening his sponge bag on the way out to reveal a bottle of holy water. It's the second week of January 1986, just after Russian Orthodox Christmas, the feast of Christ's baptism. Long ago, whole congregations processed out across the frozen water of ice-bound rivers and lakes. A hole was cut in the ice. The water was blessed. Newborn babies were dipped into it and everyone slithered home again. Nowadays, you bring empty bottles to church and top up your supply of holy water for the year. I'm not sure why one of our friends insisted that we should take this hallowed water home to Scotland, but I do know that Stuart was hard put to explain to a woman Customs official that the murky water tourists were warned not to drink was an essential part of his travel requirements!

I'd like to have had a photograph, too, of a hardback, lined jotter. It had belonged to Stuart when he was 13. He'd used the first few pages to catalogue his stamp collection, but the rest was nearly empty, so I took it with me to make notes in. The list of foreign countries excited suspicion. A heavily jowled military man stalked up to me at the Customs desk. 'Vot eez zis?' he demanded, stabbing at the list, all his chins wobbling. 'It's my husband's stamp collection when he was a little boy', I said weakly. The young official who had been dealing with me added something which I couldn't follow. The General flung the book at me and stomped away in disgust.

He might have been even more disgusted if he'd known that, among the carefully listed catalogue of stamps and countries, Stuart had just added the details of some young Baptist protestors who'd been put in prison, charged with anti-Soviet activity.

The tragedy is that it is men like him who control Russia still, men of limited vision whose careers depended on their allegiance to a system based on lies.

Those who enjoy democracy cannot comprehend life in a police state. The Russia of those years of the former Soviet Union reminded me of C. S. Lewis' Narnia under the cruel regime of the White Witch, when it was 'always winter but never Christmas'. I had no idea that wintry frosts would so soon blight the life of my then teenage daughter.

I took no photographs, but if I had done, they would have been black and white. No colour at all, not even grey. Just the white of snow and the black of people in their dark winter coats. The black of ill-lit city streets, too, during long winter nights.

On this first ever visit, I saw an endless queue of people standing out in the January snow. The bus turned a corner, and still the queue of patient, fur-clad people waited in the cold. They certainly weren't queuing for vodka. There was no shop in sight, 'What are they waiting for?' I naively asked. 'To see Lenin's body', Stuart told me.

I couldn't believe it! Queuing to view a corpse! I understood then that the old Soviet Empire was rotten at the core: at its heart was a body preserved and embalmed, but dead.

People still queue to see the long-dead leader, but time has marched on and, in 1989, we responded warmly to an invitation to give talks to a small group of Orthodox Christians in Leningrad who were now meeting officially for the first time. All in all, this three-week visit was full of surprises. Out of those discussions came a decision of great moment for us: we decided to move to Russia from our parish in Edinburgh where Stuart had served for the past seven years as a Scottish Episcopal priest. But something else happened to me. I witnessed a strangely Russian miracle, one which would give me that puzzling souvenir, the blessing of sorrow. To set the event in context, I'd like to share, not a snapshot, but a poem in which Christ is seen in a Russian setting.

Son of Man

His face is crowned with candleshine,
solemnity of soaring voices,
the incense word: *pomiluj.*

He is slumped in dust
of six million trampling feet,
hat of rabbit fur askew.

Out of town we glimpse him among birches –
those naked Russian darlings –
reaching from thawing earth to distant blue.

Dark pines praise him,
bowed beneath April snow.

He is in the faces
of shawled women,
whose eyes suffer, bloodshot, bruised.

As well as in laughter of lovers
and children swaddled like bundles
in soulless cities, shabby and subdued.

Loss and Language,
Chapman Publishing, Edinburgh, 1994

Pomiluj means 'have mercy' – two words which were to be never far from my heart during the next troubled years. In 1989, I had no inkling of any great personal or family need. My friend Natasha asked me to go with her to the shrine of a woman much revered in St Petersburg, the Blessed Xenia, who had been canonized only the year before (in a country still officially atheist). Xenia was a noblewoman before the Russian Revolution of 1917. Widowed at 20 and childless, she devoted her life to the poor. Miracles of divine healing began to be attributed to her and, after her death, even under Stalin, people in need gathered around her grave to pray. A small chapel was built around the tomb.

Of course I agreed and Natasha and I set off together across the city to Basil Island, *Vasilievsky Ostrov*. There was to be a short service in the small chapel dedicated to Xenia. All of a sudden, all the clergy, fully robed in splendid vestments, swept into the church, crushing us lay people back against the wall. 'Didn't you see him, didn't you see him?' a woman asked after the service. And my friend explained that a *staretz*, an elder, had just arrived.

A *staretz* is a monk who lives beyond the confines of any monastery and certainly outside the confines of a State which required its citizens to live only where they were legally registered. Officially these holy men (and women) no longer exist. In fact, their hidden lives, totally anonymous, all but wiped out, have continually revived the Church. Leading lives of great secrecy, they kept faith alive in a nation where it had been driven underground, and their hidden prayers may be the reason faith hasn't been completely extinguished in the secular West as well.

In our publicity conscious age, not much is hidden. Advertise or no one will come. People who don't exist officially have no way to advertise, yet hundreds come.

It was in honour of this hermit monk that the clergy put on splendid vestments to sweep into the little church that day.

In Russia, people have always travelled great distances, in hilly country or deep into the forests, to receive spiritual counsel and blessing from the hermit monks and nuns. Many have spiritual gifts: they know peoples' needs before they are spoken of and give words of prophecy as well as of encouragement or admonition. People are healed by their touch. When religious life was almost totally suppressed, many of these men and women perished in the camps, but they did not lose their faith. Their witness encouraged prisoners who had nothing to look forward to except exhaustion and death. People, and especially the young, still flock to them like bees to blossom, to draw forth sweetness and joy from men so thin with fasting their bodies seem hardly rooted to this earth.

Now, the rumour went round, the *staretz* was outside the chapel. He would bless us, the women. Would I, asked my friend, like to receive his blessing? I agreed. It was the beginning of my journey.

Ancient literature is full of journeys and the Bible is no exception. To mention just one: when unwed Mary heard the news that she was to be mother of the One who would save Israel and gave her assent, she made a journey. Luke, the Gospel writer, tells us, matter-of-factly, 'Mary got ready and hurried off to a town in the hill-country of Judea. She went into Zechariah's house and greeted Elizabeth' (Luke 1.39, 40, *Good News Bible*).

These few words don't tell us how Mary travelled, nor how long the journey lasted. We can easily imagine that it wasn't easy.

In fact, we are always being called to journey. All through the 2000 years of the Christian story, we trace the travelling of pilgrim people. The Celtic Christians, for example, whose spirituality has a common source with that of the gaunt hermit-monk who had come to Leningrad that day, were always making journeys in their little leather boats over wild seas. They called it the 'White Martyrdom'. There are hundreds of accounts of these journeys. One of my favourites originates in a ninth-century Irish manuscript. I put it into a poem, which is particularly poignant for me now because so many young people, like Elaine, start off on the voyage of life with courage and high hopes and find themselves shipwrecked on the way. Here, a young person wonders whether or not to brave the unknown.

The Question

Musicians came to the hall last night,
unpacking sagas and songs.
Harp music rippled like the burn in spate
baptizing old battles and wrongs.

A boy slipped outside.
'King of the Mysteries, shall I leave
chariots and honour, passion and pride
for an uncertain boat and the sea's grey heave?'

Rocks raised question marks
on the parchment of the tide. 'Who will make
this journey with me among currents and sharks?
King, Christ, will I take

your song in my coracle over the sea?
Will I rest with you as I lie at night
on birch without eiderdown? Hard sanctity!
Will I choose holiness without fame or delight

to build a church of driftwood and turf,
and preach to mackerel and gulls?
For the wave and for you, Bright King,
  leave the hearth,
the hall and the harp, the mead and the girls?

Loss and Language, Chapman Publishing, Edinburgh, 1994

It can happen that our journey is to stay at home and explore the complicated, dangerous territory of the heart and the emotions – and that can be a harder journey to make. But whether the voyage is physical or not, journeying involves a casting off, a leaving behind.

Young Mary's journey took her to her kinswoman, Elizabeth. There is great rejoicing in the mutual support of these two women, and now, in Communist Leningrad, Natasha was rejoicing with me over the marvellous event which had taken place – the coming of the solitary monk.

If I had taken a photograph, it would have shown us both shawled in those typical flowery scarves Russian women bind around their heads when they attend church. Beneath brown buds barely beginning to unfurl the first fronds of fresh green stood a man in a brown habit. He wore a plain wooden cross around his neck. Natasha led me to him. 'This is a pastor's wife from Scotland,' she said, highlighting my non-Orthodoxy and my foreignness. 'She doesn't speak much Russian.'

My journey was only a few steps, but it took me beyond the perceived understanding of much Western Christianity.

The shrunken brown man took my head into his hands and cradled it against him. 'The Lord bless you,' he said. 'The Lord bless you.' And in welcoming me thus, the *staretz* had made a journey, too, out of the prejudices of Orthodoxy, which denies pluralism and describes the non-Orthodox as non-Christian.

Traffic roared in the distance. The unexpected encounter was nothing short of a miracle – me, a Western woman, and the hidden Russian monk – yet there was no outward show, nothing of moment. The *staretz* blessed Natasha too and we both walked away, slowly, not wanting to rush back to busy city life, savouring what had happened. Natasha was jubilant. 'He blessed me in the usual way, just laying his hand on my head, but he took your head into his hands. He rocked you against him like a child.' I agreed. I too felt as though something really wonderful had happened to me. I wanted to cry. I wanted to relive that moment, but it had gone for ever.

That autumn, Elaine took to her bed. She had been living in a friend's flat, but, like an injured bird, like a small hurt creature, she returned home. She attempted an overdose. I cannot yet, seven years later, pass without horror the point we were driving past when she told me that she had, two weeks before, tried to kill herself. At first I was too shocked to take it in. Then, 'Thank God you didn't succeed,' I said.

Thereafter, she shut herself in her bedroom. She had become estranged, hostile, accusatory, because this was the way the world had become to her, exactly as she described it earlier. But none of us understood. In all those months of her isolation, as I approached her closed door, I made the sign of the cross and I thought, 'Where is the blessing of the *staretz*? Where *is* the blessing of the *staretz*?'

Much later I shared this story with a friend. By then I knew the diagnosis.

'Your daughter is very unwell and may never live a normal life', a hospital consultant told Stuart and me, bluntly.

We stared at him. Yes, she was unwell. That's why she was in hospital, but hospitals are supposed to make you better, aren't they? So, what was the man saying, 'may never live a normal life'?

'But what's the matter with her?' we stammered.

'She has a schizophrenic illness.' That was all. Perhaps he tried to describe schizophrenia to us, I don't remember – I was far too stunned. What I do know is that there were no words of comfort – what words can there be? No explanation of what treatment – if any – the hospital was offering. No information about help groups, nothing – just this one cold statement of fact.

Where was the blessing of the *staretz*? My friend had an answer. 'The *staretz* blessed you with sorrow, for sorrow is also a blessing.' And he quoted words of Ignatius Loyola: 'your sorrows are your blessings for they do shelter you in the wounds of Christ'.

The souvenir I have been given on the journey I make with my daughter is the blessing of a Russian monk, the blessing of sorrow.

CHAPTER 2

Mountains of the Mind

Her name isn't really Elaine. Her real name means 'little bright spark' and she lived up to it – full of fun, a total mimic with a genius for accents, and for getting her own quiet way. Her brother was the tempestuous, uproarious one. Beside him she seemed possessed by an inner serenity, tender-hearted and gentle.

When she was a baby, we lived in York and once we went to Whitby and scrambled up grassy slopes beside the sea. It was early spring and, out of the wind, the sun was warm. She was wrapped up in a little furry suit with a hood – pale blue because it had been passed down from her brother. We called it her seal suit. I laid her in a hollow of the cliffs and her quiet eyes looked up at me as I told her that the world is a beautiful place. I couldn't have told it to a better person. She grew up attuned to beauty. She loves our holiday place on the far-flung shores of the west.

It was her eyes my mother first noticed. My mother had Parkinson's disease. Typically, Parkinson's disease affects older people, but she was relatively young – she was 55 and my twin sister and I were 19 when her illness was diagnosed. Not long after, I heard a radio programme about Parkinson's and a patient who had lost the power of speech. I thought, 'That won't ever happen to my mother', but it did. By the time my children were born,

17

she could hardly talk at all. But sometimes little things sparked her into response and when we carried our four-month-old baby daughter, her only granddaughter, into the house and put her down, she bent unsteadily over the cot. 'Oh, what a beautiful baby!' she said. 'What beautiful eyes.'

It was my mother's Parkinson's which first gave me some inkling about schizophrenia. I used to think, bathing, feeding her, that what Parkinson's does for the body's movements, schizophrenia must do for the mind.

Both diseases are to do with a chemical called dopamine. In Parkinson's, the level of dopamine in the brain is reduced. It's thought, however, that schizophrenia is caused by the dopamine receptors getting snarled up so that too much of this chemical is received by the brain cells. Neuroleptic drugs reduce paranoia by blocking the dopamine receptors and can, alas, produce the rigidity and tremor of Parkinson's disease as well as a flattening out of emotion, whereas the drugs used to control Parkinson's can result in the paranoia and hallucinations of schizophrenia.

One night I noticed a weal across my mother's shoulder, caused by the friction of the sling she had been wearing because she had broken her arm after one of her frequent falls. It must have been bothering her all day and yet she had never complained. The words flashed into my head, 'Blessed are the meek, for they shall inherit the earth'.

My children were small then. Elaine was four, her brother was six. We were staying at my parents' house in Glasgow. I took them to a nearby park where there was a small boating pond. The pond was so little and the boats so stable that even very young children were able to operate them alone.

I sat on a brick in the lee of a tumbledown building and watched the wind ruffle the water, whip colour into two happy faces.

I found myself writing a poem. I'd written stories when I was small, then 'novels', and I had already begun to publish my work, but as far as poetry was concerned I was right at the beginning, feeling my way. As I groped with ideas and words, I felt that my poem should be a sonnet. It had been so long since I had studied poetry that I couldn't at first recall the correct form, but as I worked, scoring out, tapping out metre, it came back.

Instead of a photograph from the family album of this time, I should like to share the last three lines of the poem I wrote for my mother that windy March day.

Sometimes with humour and with rare, glad grace
you leave your cage and, though you hardly speak,
you own the heritage bequeathed the meek.

I understood that there were connections between Parkinson's disease and schizophrenia, but I never, never guessed that an illness of the mind would cripple my daughter.

Because of the high prevalence of schizophrenia, because patients are no longer locked away in forbidding Victorian hospitals and because of media coverage, people know about this illness through hearsay or through the experience of 'a friend of a friend'. Churches which have become informal enough to be accepting of people who might wander in late or get up and leave early will also have in their congregation people who suffer from mental illness.

The first factual information I ever had about schizophrenia was on a potted course of psychiatry. We were told that mental illness divides broadly into two categories: neurotic and psychotic. In neurotic illnesses, reality may become unbearable, but patients don't lose touch with the real world. In psychotic illnesses, however, the reverse is true – criss-crossed thoughts become reality.

'I was feeling worse and worse about myself,' wrote Elaine in her first letter home to us in Edinburgh from her year in Seville, 1987, 'and feeling more and more unhappy, till eventually I cracked in a church service and I started sobbing hysterically like I've never done before. . . .'

In another letter, she wrote about feeling 'oppressed' and, later, describing the family where she worked as a nanny, she wrote:

> The children are lovely. Nataniel knows my name and calls me 'ainy' or 'lainy'. Baby Samuel is lovely too. Some of their relatives have regarded me suspiciously. Two of them came up when I was looking after the bairns and Nataniel had just done a big jobi and they made a big event about how he was smelly and how horrible it was to be sitting in jobi. And then in church I couldn't stop the baby crying and some relative came and grabbed the baby without a word and of course shut it up. I felt terrible!!

This idea of being regarded with suspicion was a recurring theme in her letters. Another one, also in 1987, gives a second description of 'something funny which came over me'.

> It was the English service in the morning but there was something about it that annoyed me and in the service at evening something funny came over me and I started crying for no reason, but of course I

didn't want anyone to see, so I choked back the tears. All I wanted to do was run out, but I stuck it out till the end without participating, and as soon as it finished I rushed out without saying cheerio to anybody, leaving everybody wondering what was wrong. I don't know what came over me.

On the whole, her letters were lively with little details like, 'we had *caldito* and *pabillas* (Spanish snacks) for lunch today; and the girl who cut my hair in the *academia* (hairdressing college) I discovered was a guy – he was a transvestite and I didn't even realize!'

I've been sitting on the balcony of my block of flats amongst the washing writing letters in the sun. It's got really hot and it's only March. There's a wee man that's always out on the balcony looking at everything with his binoculars, including me! People still continue staring at me all the time and shouting, 'Rubia!' (blondie). It's so annoying. . . . Someone was playing the piano and the music went mingling down the street with all the other sounds: kids playing football, the man with his wee flute and his cart to let people know he's there to sharpen their knives. This morning gypsies came by with their trumpets and drums and a goat perched on a stepladder on a brick and a monkey tied to a chain. . . .

The photographs from Seville show an attractive, tall, slim girl standing under an orange tree smiling at a baby in her arms or gracefully dancing the traditional flamenco dance, her arms raised as she twirls. But one photograph shows her facing the camera. Her eyes are narrowed. Her expression is shuttered, suspicious, closed. 'You're not looking very happy in that one', I commented.

With hindsight, we realize that this sadness, the feeling of being regarded with suspicion, were early signs of what was to come. But what exactly is schizophrenia?

It's generally agreed to be a whole series of behaviours resulting from a disorder of the mind which affects thoughts, feelings and, eventually, all aspects of daily living. It typically occurs in the late teens or early twenties. Nearly 1 person in 100 worldwide will develop schizophrenia at some time in their lives – a very high incidence, not least when it's multiplied by the number of families of sufferers who share the devastation. Almost every piece of scientific literature I've come across admits that this illness is 'poorly understood' and that treatment remains 'unsatisfactory'.

The title of this chapter – Mountains of the Mind – comes from a sonnet by Gerard Manley Hopkins. I discovered that poem when I was 17, a formative year for me. The world was at spring, all a fresh burgeoning of delight, 'charged with the grandeur of God', as Hopkins himself puts it, who also praised all 'dappled things'.

Although life was definitely to be delighted in, I felt a special concern for people whose young lives had been messed up by World War II and, when I was 19, at the end of my first year at university, I worked in Northern Germany among so-called 'displaced persons' – people without passport or nation who were too sick to take part in the economic boom which was just beginning to take off in their host country.

The people I met were from countries I'd barely heard of – Latvia, Lithuania, as well as very many people from Poland. Many had been forcibly taken from their families and brought to Germany as slave labourers. Others had been concentration camp victims. Others had been trapped in West Germany in the melting pot of nations in 1945 when the map of Europe was redrawn by the people at the top.

I came back to Glasgow determined to learn Polish, so I pricked up my ears when I heard a student say to someone that he'd just been to Poland. That student was Stuart. We met him in the last chapter being searched by the KGB! My first snapshots of him show him with lots of curly hair and a beardless chin. Now he has a beard like a grey squirrel and a big bald head.

'Would you like to learn Polish?' he asked. Those were almost his first words to me – and they sealed our relationship! We spent a postgraduate year in Poland back in the sixties and have been privileged to make a few short trips there since.

Much more recently, in 1990, I went on a tour of Poland with a small group of Scottish folksingers and poets. At one point we stayed outside a town called Opole in what had once been Germany. Untended gravestones in the churchyard were written in German. I wondered what might have happened to the ethnic German people who had once ploughed and harvested those quiet fields. I assumed that when Poland's borders were shifted west in 1945 they had all been resettled in Germany. It was only later when I saw a television documentary that I learnt what their fate had been. Germans were victims, too. I made them the subject of a poem.

Ethnic Cleansing, Western Poland 1945

Film. The few survivors do not speak.
Their no words say it all.

These haunted eyes still look on hell –
it was a lifetime ago,
and they were forbidden to tell.

But in villages
where storks build high nests,
I have seen abandoned gravestones,
mute legacy of a vanished race
who called this land their own.

Until generals played their ruthless chess;
and maps were redrawn.

Victims of war find the fabric of their lives split apart.
And that is what schizophrenia feels like to the sufferer:
an internal catastrophe which destroys the fabric of
being.

Because of my happiness in my late teens, it was an
added sorrow for me that my lovely daughter spent those
sweet years walled up in her room. I learnt the truth of
Hopkins' poem. The mountains of the mind indeed are
'no-man-fathomed'.

In my attempt to come to terms with what had happened to Elaine, I took notes from a book of psychiatry.
It had been three years since Elaine's first spell in a mental
hospital and we had still been given no coherent information about the illness which had taken hold of our
daughter. Elaine was living in what is called supported
accommodation. She was very happy there and, for the first
time in three years, was being consistently maintained
on medication thanks to regular visits from a community

psychiatric nurse – an absolutely vital link in the lives of patients with an illness of the mind who live in 'the community'.

By then, Stuart and I were living full time in Russia, coming home to Edinburgh for the summer. That year we were given the use of our old rectory, which had been our home for all Elaine's teenage years. Elaine came round to see us. I'm always nagging her about smoking and I'd picked up leaflets about nicotine patches. She brushed them aside. But she had news for me. 'Talking about leaflets, Mum,' she said, 'I've just been reading one. I've got schizophrenia. God must hate me to do that to me.'

It was the first time she'd talked so directly about her illness. I felt very encouraged, feeling we were on the right track at last. 'Come and have a cup of coffee,' I invited. 'Let's sit outside.' So, here's a photograph of us now. We're in the back garden of our old rectory. After Elaine's first spell in hospital in 1991, she had a period of immense creativity. She painted, sewed and gardened. Our garden had never looked so nice! She planted gladioli and various shrubs, which provided a background to us, sitting reading the leaflet together. Then I said, rather hesitantly. 'I've been reading about schizophrenia, too. It's in a book for medical students. It's a bit heavy. Would you like to see it?'

Elaine read the relevant pages without comment as we sat side by side in the garden. It was almost as though she blanked out what she was reading, but then she spotted the next section and seized upon it. It was on grief. 'This is what's happened to me', she said. She had repeatedly told us that she had lost part of herself and, of course, we didn't understand at the time.

But in seizing so eagerly on what seemed to her to be

explanations for the black experiences she had undergone, she was already moving away from her admission that the disease known as schizophrenia was what she was suffering from. It was like watching a shutter fall, and I've seen it happen time and again.

I have to say that the textbook prognosis is bleak for someone like our daughter who became affected as young as her teens (as we now understand) and in whom the illness progressed slowly. Looking back, we see that as early as 16 she may have been showing symptoms. She would sleep for inordinate amounts of time, day and night. We thought it was because she was growing still and needed extra sleep. We called her our dormouse, our Sleeping Beauty.

That's why I've entitled this book *Uninvited Guest*. Remember the Bad Fairy who came uninvited to Briar Rose's christening and pronounced 'At 16 the princess will prick herself on a spindle and die'? Then the Good Fairy stepped forward and softened the Bad Fairy's wish. That Good Fairy would once upon a time have been called a godsib, someone invited to the christening with a specific role in the newborn baby's life as part of the baby's extended family – in this case, a vital one: the turning aside of ill.

People ask me if there were signs when Elaine was a baby. There were none. She was outgoing and sociable. At five, she was taken by her Grandma to a family wedding. Fair-haired Elaine swished in her long pink dress to the top-hatted father of the bride. 'You haven't any dances for little girls', she pointed out. The bride's father spoke to the band leader. The band struck up 'The Grand old Duke of York' and Elaine and her host took the floor and led the wedding party in the dance.

So, no, we had no idea of what awaited us. Without being studious or seeming academic, Elaine won prizes for writing, for art. Our family album includes a photograph of Elaine, a sweet-faced nine-year-old girl in a blue anorak standing in front of her prizewinning drawing in the Royal Scottish Museum.

We took one of her brother, too. He can't draw, but he was great at making a noise. He's standing in front of a stuffed tiger, his open mouth mirroring the tiger's unvoiced roar.

Elaine was agile and moves and dances well. She swam well, too, and took part in synchronized swimming, a highly co-ordinated activity.

When she was nine, we had daughters of Spanish friends to stay. Elaine was so thrilled by this contact with another language that she began to study Spanish. When she was 13, she travelled alone to Spain and stayed with this pair of older girls. The next year, she went back alone and stayed with different friends, friends of her great friend, Carol. We had no idea then what an important role Carol would play in our lives. Nor, as I have said, had we any idea about the time-bomb which was about to explode in our family, about the presence of the 'uninvited guest', the lurking gene which would so totally ground our talented daughter. I have used the image of someone grounded in the next poem. It was provoked by a letter from a friend in Russia, complaining that she felt boxed in and could see no way out. Schizophrenia hems a young person in, cutting off their options. A friend who knew Elaine well, pre-illness, and was as devastated as us by the diagnosis, put it this way: 'Elaine aspired to such heights. She was like Icarus, the boy who flew too close to the sun'.

A Sparrow's Flight

'St Petersburg is a dead end – but what
is in Crimea, home, once Paradise,
a sun-steeped playground, rich in vine and fruit,
sad symbol now of soviet demise,'
a student wrote. 'No future there – or here.
I'm stuck: a moth in amber petrifies –
like souls too frail to win through mirk and mire.'

My daughter's hurt is seen in haunted eyes.
She too is stuck; and voices, demons jeer.
For if: 'We thought our life a sparrow's flight
from dark to dark, we knew not whence nor where
save this brief sojourn in feast and firelight . . .'
she, brilliant, shone too near the searing flame,
then fell in ash and shadow, grounded, maimed.

A huge fog of folklore surrounds schizophrenia. Psychiatrists generally regard this disease as being one in which medication is all-essential. Psychologists may say it's a cognitive overload and needs to be dealt with by rational discussion. Sociologists say it's to do with a dislocated world. Sufferers, who, typically, fail to understand that they have an illness, believe they are being persecuted by psychiatrists as much as by the black thoughts which can drive them to self-mutilation and, indeed, suicide.

Elaine's brother is a research worker, but, to my dismay, he's a biker. He not only rides motor bikes, he races them. He has a book about track techniques which warns that 'survival instincts are dangerous'. Riders are persuaded to master their basic sense of fear.

Elaine feels that her very survival is threatened. 'People don't realize that I have to live with fewer resources and less confidence than they do', she points out repeatedly.

My next poem uses motor bike racing to highlight aspects of schizophrenia.

Overdrive

Her biker brother's racing handbooks state,
don't trust survival instincts to negate
the risk of hurt. Helmet and leather gear,
well-planned tactics protect far more than fear.
To keep top speed, extend and dip the knee –
you graze the ground, but note: the human bone
is weak, may break beneath a mere three stone,
so ride and learn your limit is the key.

Yet when the brain goes into overdrive
no tricks of track can help the self survive;
no cambered roadway keeps rash thoughts on course,
just drugs and needles – if need be, by force.

The psyche's pitch is finely tuned, refined:
no physic's found to mend a broken mind.

Elaine says she feels as though she's living in a cage, as though mind and body both were 'an empty cage' and there was no escape. And she added, 'I spend most of my time striving not to live in isolation, not to be in a cage. The only thing that brings me near to what I used to be is praising God. I used to think that if I strove to make things better, God would help me out, but often he just leaves me in it.'

We were sitting in her high-rise flat. The wind swept around her window. She smiled and said, 'I love the wind. It reminds me of the sea, of being away on the west coast among the sand dunes. And it makes me think of God.' 'I'm sure you're nearer to God than most of us, Elaine,' I replied.

My textbook notes that where there is thought disorder, social withdrawal, a deterioration from a previous level of functioning, the 'diagnosis of schizophrenia has to be considered'.

One of the first things we noticed which puzzled us about Elaine's behaviour, besides prolonged, unexplained weeping, was that whenever we were all together around the table as a family, she would fall silent. I suppose that's the 'social withdrawal' the textbook mentions.

Later I read that families don't cause schizophrenia, but that the chemistry of a family can affect the course of the illness. If you put too much pressure on the person, get too entangled in their life, that's bad. There's a fine line between encouragement and 'nagging', however, and we were groping in the dark. I persuaded Elaine to see a counsellor who later phoned me and said, 'Elaine needs your time and company.' So I intruded behind her closed door, brought her meals on a tray, sat with her while she ate, waited on her hand and foot – and made matters worse.

Elaine now says no, I didn't make things worse at all. Recently she was lying alone in bed and, as she put it, 'wanting to be secluded'. She recalled those 'meals on wheels' I had brought into her room in those years before the diagnosis and, looking back, she felt that I had made her feel less isolated during those years of being secluded in her bedroom.

Slowly, over many years, we learnt the vital facts: a person who suffers from schizophrenia needs space and a stress-free environment. After all, someone with a broken leg isn't expected to run a marathon. But when the mind is broken, 'no tricks of track can keep the self alive'.

Our family album at that time isn't a happy one. One photograph shows Elaine with her hair beautifully styled, but her eyes are hostile. The following extract from my diary sums up this fraught time.

We coincide at around 1.30 – my lunch, her breakfast. She speaks pleasantly, but as we sit in the same room in silence, no topic is safe to raise – she turns on me a look of such contempt I'm forced to say, 'What is it?'

She replies, 'You've destroyed me, taken my life away, sent people after me when I was ill. What will you do at my funeral? Laugh. You'll give me a donkey's funeral and no one will come . . . Mothers are meant to be mothers not persecutors . . .' I know I ought to get up and walk away, but I'm stunned. I feel as though a nail has been driven through me, keeping me pinned down. She gets a book and holds it threateningly over me, but throws it on to the floor instead with a cry, 'God help me.' Then she turns her back, hunched over the paper, with job applications. My presence in her life is a constant source of anger. I go upstairs, paralysed emotionally and in tears which I've managed not to show her. I do all I can to keep a low profile in her life. There is no way forward.

We've had to learn to recast our perceptions of our daughter, and that's what the following poem illustrates.

Drawing Class

'I can't draw a cat,' she said,
wiping out her third attempt,
'until I know its anatomy.'

Tutored thus, I understood
I had not studied the bones
on which I fleshed my trust.

Amateurs assume too much;
a botched-up job does for the real thing.

The artist stands back
– and starts again.

Typically the onset of schizophrenia is so slow that when relatives turn to outsiders for help, they've really reached their wits' end. Once, when it was all too much for me, I ran to the doctor in tears. I begged him to give me a sleeping pill, a bed in hospital, anything to give me respite. The doctor thrust a box of tissues at me, listened sympathetically for almost an hour and told me I was carrying too much guilt. He said we needed to draw limitations around our daughter and if she failed to conform, we should put her out.

'Put her out'! Where would she go? She was vulnerable and totally lacking in self-esteem, no hope. There was no way you could simply make her 'buck up and get on with it'.

The Schizophrenia Association of Great Britain (SAGB) points out that doctors are not prepared to diagnose schizophrenia until severe symptoms develop: paranoia, delusions, thought disorder. 'With all other diseases it is thought to be of huge importance to diagnose as early as possible so that treatment can start and deterioration be prevented. The opposite occurs in schizophrenia.

Deterioration of the illness is waited for and, when it occurs, it is less easy to treat.' (*Can You Tell Me Something About Schizophrenia?*, SAGB.)

That was exactly our experience. Over and over again we heard doctors say that Elaine was simply failing to make the break into adult life and was therefore turning back to an angry, more infantile stage of development. No one, however, predicted when this stage might end and a breakthrough into 'normal' life would occur.

A counsellor told us, 'You are a sick family. Elaine is bearing your symptoms.' Our first consultation with a psychiatrist wasn't much better.

Elaine had locked herself in the bathroom at midnight, ransacked the whole bathroom until she found a razor (I had removed everything I could think of which she might use to harm herself – we had no aspirins in our house all those years). She cut her wrists, sobbing. Standing outside the bathroom, wondering why she was taking so long, my son and I reacted immediately. He broke the lock. I phoned for an ambulance and we were taken to casualty where they bandaged what was really only a superficial wound. But at least from that we got a referral to see a psychiatrist the next morning.

The psychiatrist, not much older than Elaine, talked to her, then called us in together and said, 'Why don't you take up jogging?'

I was furious! I'd gone without sleep, phoned ten people to cancel a class I was taking and sought her professional advice. You don't need a degree in psychiatry to advise 'take up jogging'! Did the woman think I hadn't made an endless nuisance of myself all winter, phoning people in church and begging, 'Oh, do include Elaine', who wasn't well enough to be included.

In all this darkness, a star. It was the love of our neighbours, Chris and Gwynneth. We returned from that midnight drive to casualty to find a note on our door: 'If you need us, knock us up, no matter what time it is.' And often afterwards, those friends would invite us in for supper. They never said much, but they let us talk. When we left, their hugs showed how much they cared. I have never forgotten the unspoken love, understanding and care in those embraces.

It was after that attempt to slash her wrists that Elaine poured out her feelings on paper in what she has called her 'post-suicide note'. Her words are particularly poignant to me, partly because of the pain they reveal but also because it is the last piece of sustained creative work that Elaine was ever to achieve, apart from some paintings, which she did sobbing as she worked, and the gardening she later undertook.

After the consultation, Elaine attended hospital as an out-patient for a further three months. It was another year before she was finally admitted as an in-patient. Another whole year of her young life had gone. But even then, even having been given a diagnosis, help was not forth-coming. Medication was prescribed in tablet form, which Elaine refused to take. Those all-important tablets lay untouched beside her bed. She lay in bed until *Neighbours* at 1.30. I never guessed I would be grateful for a soap, but it got our daughter out of bed!

And afterwards she just lay on the settee.

What comfort can parents offer each other? We were often in tears. Or else we vented our anger and frustration on each other. One night I heard Stuart weeping. I didn't even put out my hand to comfort him. It had got beyond comfort. All our hopes had been dashed. Elaine's lack of volition, inability to organize her life, withdrawal – these are classic symptoms. And up until now no medication has been found to treat this aspect of the illness.

She needed structure, the doctor agreed, but who would give it to her, how was she to get it?

I wrote wearily in my diary, 'Flesh and spirit ache from this scourge.'

And still we had very little understanding of what was going on inside her mind. Once I was passing through the kitchen where she was sitting having coffee with a friend. She pushed a box of matches across the table. It must have said something about 'conforming to safety requirements'. Elaine pointed to the word 'conform'. 'That's what I have to do,' she said. 'I see that word every time I light a cigarette.'

This seems to be typical of her illness. Words, advertisements, slogans sometimes carry immense significance. They have to be obeyed in some way. Sometimes it can seem as though the television is a special messenger, speaking in some significant way, either threatening her or warning her about the presence of those who may harm her.

Since then, Stuart and I have spent some time in Finland. This small country of lakes and forests has, like Scotland, a population of only five million. People spend their holidays in 'summer cottages' on lake shores and islands. If you go to Finland and take a boat out on those quiet lakes, here's a tip. Don't sail too close to the islands. We did, and the residents of the little wooden house on the shore – father, mother, child – turned their bare backsides hastily towards us. You go naked from the sauna into the lake!

Finnish friends have told me that there is a high incidence of mental illness in their country. They were shocked to hear of our struggles to keep Elaine on medication. Recognizing, as the Schizophrenia Association of Great Britain leaflet states, that early and continuous treatment is vital, the practice in Finland is to keep a patient in in-treatment care for a full three months until they are well-established on medication and only then allow them home on very gradual visits, firstly for a few hours, then a day, then overnight, a weekend and so on. Yet Elaine had been discharged from hospital with a prescription for medication she saw no reason to take and we watched her become more isolated and helpless day after day.

We're a terrible family for losing keys. We sit on doorsteps for hours waiting for someone to let us in, we climb through open windows. Once I locked myself out on the very day Stuart had gone off for 24 hours. So it wasn't unusual when I lost the car key. And, of course, the car was immobilized. We hurried and scurried around Elaine, who was totally ignoring us all, taking no part in the frantic search. Where, I wondered, is the key to restore her mobility? Her doors were so firmly shut, all solutions out of reach. Is harmony possible, I wondered sadly, or was it just a bitter dream?

I begged a GP to call and bring tablets, not just a prescription. The doctor did indeed call and persuaded Elaine to take a tablet. We saw an immediate improvement. After being buffeted by despair, I tried to cling on to the comfort that our family is still together despite the anguish of these last years.

We had found the missing key, but Elaine stopped her medication and the GP refused to visit again. 'She's 21,' she told me sternly. 'It's her choice whether she's ill or not. You, Mrs Robertson, have to stand back from it and watch her deteriorate. . . . She knows she can come to us when she needs help.' But the whole problem with schizophrenia is that the patient doesn't know that she is ill. She doesn't understand she needs help.

And so I was stymied once again. I watched my lovely

girl sink back into apathy. As she lay on the settee with her back turned to me, I sat down on my favourite bean-bag, picked up a paper and read, 'The risen Christ appeared when the doors were locked'. Those words provoked the poem which ends this chapter.

The Wound in Your Mind

Rowan berries tinge the bright years of your lost
   girlhood.
You tell me beauty has a bitter taste.

A secret smile flickers across your face.
When you speak – your words are sharp with hurt.

The wound in your mind refuses love.

There is no key, you are locked in, fast.

The sea is a wild dream, a madness of foam . . .

My swan princess . . . yours the pools and islands
   of the west:
                                    fly again.

Loss and Language, Chapman Publishing, Edinburgh, 1994

CHAPTER 3

'Sometimes I fear
I'm losing my mind'

Elaine was certain that her year in Spain had somehow messed up her personal development. This is how her analysis of herself continues.

While I was in Spain every sentence had to be rehearsed so it would come out correctly. My initial frustration at not understanding all that was said relaxed until I got to the point where I virtually understood everything. By that stage I was continuously listening to everything and virtually only talking when spoken to. I suppose subconsciously I slipped into a kind of 'puppet on a string' role, a feeling of existing only for performance. I was often left out of conversations simply because I was a foreigner. I had to break down these barriers with every new person I met. The way in which I was constantly stared at in the streets would perhaps have helped produce an element of paranoia in any normal individual. I wore dark sunglasses to make myself look more inconspicuous and it probably did make me feel slightly abnormal at times, like a Martian on Earth. The green horns and the six eyes miraculously dropped off on returning home!

I was constantly absorbing, listening and taking in

my surroundings. Everything was new and I met so many different people. Friends used to laugh and say that I was like a small child with new shoes. The learning of the language was an exciting daily challenge, although perhaps it was more draining than I realized. I pressured myself into always improving. I absorbed the culture and the language and began to feel so much more a part of things. Sometimes I felt like a goldfish in a bowl that everybody gave their attention to and sometimes I felt like a person looking in on an aquarium full of different plants, rocks, colours and fish, and occasionally the odd fish would turn and give me a brief glance.

I came home for Christmas feeling quite Spanish. I suffered culture shock for the first few days but, nevertheless, I enjoyed being home and I was welcomed back by everyone. I spent an exciting two weeks seeing everyone and catching up on news. When it came around to time for going back I wasn't particularly enthusiastic. I felt a strange sense of foreboding about the whole idea.

When I got there I realized once again that I was now a foreigner and that *communication* involved effort. I now lived on the other side of the city. I was staying with a Spanish family and I felt cut off from the British group I had known. My social activities were curtailed. I felt distanced from everything and, probably for the first time in my life, I felt quite lonely. I was not given specific duties to do or specific working hours which I was not happy about but powerless to change. I felt like a dogsbody tagging along behind the wife, moving about the house, trying to look useful and find something useful to do. I never felt relaxed as I never knew if I was supposed to be working or not. I couldn't settle. I never knew quite what to do when visitors came. I was never at ease because I didn't quite know what my role was: was I maid, guest, friend, family or simply just a foreign visitor? I don't think the family knew either!

Both the husband and the wife had illusions of speaking fluent English by the time I left, but they weren't prepared to go through the drudgery that learning a foreign language involves. The man had the attitude that if I could speak Spanish, then he could learn English in the flick of a lamb's tail. Of course he never did and he seemed to resent me for that.

He seemed jealous of any outside contact I had and tried to cut it down to a minimum. On nights I was allowed out, it was never to be very late, which was preposterous considering Spanish culture, which involves people stopping work at 8–9 p.m., then having supper and never usually going out till 10–10.30 p.m. I saw this as unfair, but had to accept it. He disliked any friends I introduced him to and if any of them were male he insinuated that I was having affairs with them (which was extremely unjust).

Gone were the 3 o'clock in the morning walks along the river or the touring of the nicest bars or the weekend trips to other parts of Andalusía, the pleasant lunchtimes with the English or Americans I had got to know in my first three months in Seville, gone was the choosing a lunchtime meal and preparing it with my English friend and flatmate, Sharon, the mid-morning coffee breaks and chats when we both finished work and the baby was sleeping, nipping next door to the neighbours for a coffee, chatting with the man in the corner shop, talking with the girls in the street, afternoon sessions of sunbathing in the park, suppertime and then out at night.

No, this was not the same. My new employer even

resented me going to visit English friends on my so-called day off. I began to dislike him and his domineering attitude to his wife and his need to strive for power. The wife was very subdued and uneasy and often felt ill from becoming overtired and stressed, probably due to his constant demands on her. The baby was suffering from severe colic and cried a lot which made him angry, the wife became more anxious and I was left feeling more unhappy and unrelaxed. I began to feel tense even sitting next to the man at the end of a day to watch the telly (by that time my concentration span was lapsing and I had to strain to watch and understand everything). He was jealous of how much mail I received. I began to feel bad about everything.

My eyes became sore (due to stress). I then felt ill for a week with a high temperature. The doctor came and went and the husband came into the room with a big smarmy grin on his face.

By this stage I really wanted to come home, realizing I hadn't been happy from the moment I'd arrived. I missed out on a trip to the east coast through lack of money, which was disappointing – I'd pinned my hopes on it as a break away from the situation, which he gloated over and gave me a list of critical things about the place where we were going and the programme of the weekend, saying it was just as well that I hadn't gone. I realized that whatever this man dictated, the wife and I had to jump to. I wanted to go home more than ever, but I was determined to stick it out because I'd made a commitment to them. I was waiting for visits from home. I decided to think positive, 'It wasn't all bad'. I consoled myself by building up a picture of what my life was like back at home and wished away the days.

I would like to add that I have since learnt that he caused havoc in his church – over half his congregation has now left because of him. He himself and his family have since written that they are experiencing a series of difficulties which they didn't want to divulge. Not that any of that makes me feel vindicated, but it does in a way confirm my convictions.

I'd like to finish this part by saying that none of the events I've related here are in the slightest bit blown out of proportion, nor do I fully understand for whose benefit I have felt the need to write this down, but the bad memories of this time stayed with me longer than they should have. I see now, although the overall experience was enriching and beneficial and there were a lot of happy and memorable times, it has all contributed to my present predicament.

Nothing was as I thought it would be when I came home. I mentioned before about the image that I built up of home and myself in Spain when I was looking forward to returning. Little by little, I began to see that this image was idealized and it began to crumble.

I didn't seem to manage to pick up the threads of my previous life. I was unprepared for the changes I was to encounter in people. I didn't ever quite manage to find my niche again. Things got progressively worse. I was no longer completely in control of my life and I didn't seem able to sort things out and get on with the daily grind of living. Life seems to have stopped for me somewhere back in Spain. I could find no purpose and even when I started college I wasn't aware of all the implications, didn't commit myself, did no serious studying. I didn't settle happily into new relationships, although many people extended their friendship and were keen to get to know me. I felt that I'd struggled hard at Spanish, for what? To come back and start speaking English and go on forgetting it, little by little. There was no challenge or purpose left. Apathy set in as well as depression. Life was so different here and I somehow felt estranged from it. I felt that I'd left a big part of me behind. Even in the Spanish class at college I saw no point in being there: we were just going over basics and my Spanish was on a par with the teacher's. I just had to keep my mouth shut so that others could learn this strange foreign language, which to me was so very real. This apathetic feeling pervaded every other class I attended. I was aware of jealousy from some people which reduced my confidence still further. A lot of the girls had just left school and I felt were much less experienced, etc., I could see no point in sitting around aimlessly chatting. It all seemed too easy, yet I was never at ease. I found myself switching off from conversations. I seemed to resent anyone who threatened to dominate. Gradually everybody began to seem to threaten. I felt half foreign in my own country. This is where I really began to lose sight of myself and began to feel quite hopeless.

When I received the news that I would have to catch up with studies over the summer because I hadn't attended certain classes at college or handed in enough work, I was quite shocked, but I didn't sense the urgency and, anyway, I was working, unhappily, as a childminder, which only reminded me of being held down, feeling useless, by the house in Spain. So I failed. Then the reality of failing sunk in. What was I to do now? All the implications of the failure hit home to my already depressed state. I was already feeling angry, hurt and frustrated by people and I began to pine away.

In the new session, I was given the opportunity to do the work I had not done the previous year, but I had neither the motivation nor the energy to do what had been suggested.

People began hurting me more and more. Even though I was putting so much effort into everything I said, it all seemed to come out awkward and stupid. I began to get angry at people and desperate. Why was nothing working no matter how hard I tried? Why were people not responding when all my effort was for their benefit? People should be listening to me anyway – how dare they not? I just didn't seem to be good enough any more.

With my self-image and my hope crumbling rapidly, the withdrawing process began. I felt like I was a miserable failure of a nothing. I realized, however, that I do have a whole life ahead of me that has to be lived, that does go on no matter what the circumstances were like for me, no matter whether I'd switched off and cut people off and given up because even my best didn't seem to be good enough. My life and everything else still went on (funnily enough!).

Throughout this whole process I tried to explain to people what was happening and how I was feeling, but I wasn't understanding it all myself, and certainly wasn't getting adequate answers from anyone else – hence the feeling of being let down by everybody. All the meaningful relationships that I had had been broken or ruined in some way or another. I had lost all credibility.

I began to feel suicidal and made the first attempt, of which I was bitterly ashamed. I wasn't even prepared to admit to myself how desperate I was. Even when I was drugged up to the eyeballs and being trundled along on a trolley like a carcass, feeling like

I was going to die as I heard people talking over me like I didn't even exist as a person with feelings, I was totally alert, not accepting what was happening but taking it all in. My pride would not allow me to accept it. I chatted to the night nurses and to the auxiliaries and would not allow them to treat me as a patient or order me about. I was dropping on my feet, desperately tired, yet still causing a fuss, and even when one of the nurses ordered me into bed I would not get in, behaving like a stubborn three-year-old because my pride was so, so wounded.

The next morning, I went around chatting to all the other patients as if I were the visiting clergyman doing his rounds!

I struggled on, need I say any more, until last night when I had numbed myself to the shame and so hated myself that I tried to end it all properly.

I've scribbled the following words down in a hurry, in a state of emotional frenzy.

I hate life, when I used to love it. I feel threatened by people when I used to love everyone. I feel totally wasted and burnt out at 19. I should have devoted my energy to building up a life for myself instead of wasting it on people who seemingly carry on regardless of loyalty, friendship or concern. I wonder just how many people have taken me for granted and used or manipulated me. I feel I can trust no one; and when my whole lifestyle, personality and attitude have been on the basis of total trust and openness, I don't know how to deal with that or how to protect myself.

I am only now aware of my naivety, innocence and vul-nerability — ironically when everyone else (me included) had always said how mature I was. Perhaps in one respect they were right, but in the cold light of day I see that the reverse was nearer to the truth. Was it all a front? Was I never true to myself? I tried to prove to myself and everyone else that I was not the typically stigmatized 'minister's daughter', but I have now become a Christian who does not want to be a hypocrite. Also, I despised weakness in people and yet now find myself in what I see to be a weak and pitiful state. All this makes it ten times harder to accept. I seem to be saying things that I didn't want to say all the time just to protect myself, which was horrible as I realized how my level of conversation had dropped.

I've tried everything in the past year and half to sort things out and try and improve them. I looked for reassurance but there was none. So I looked for some convincing evidence to justify my thoughts and feelings. I remained passive and silent and people became confused by my silence and commented on how I'd changed since returning from Spain. Horribly for me, I began to see how their reactions to me began to change. I felt confused and totally out of control and very frustrated by everything and, horribly, all the negative thoughts about me were justified by this.

I then tried hard to be someone and mean something to friends and family and to people in general which only left me feeling foolish as well as the desperate insecurity I was feeling. I slipped into the habit of mentally rehearsing past conversations to see what the other person had meant. I used up so much emotional energy doing this that it's no wonder I ended up feeling drained. The self-doubt set in. Nothing came out spontaneously and communication became an effort. It became like it had been in Spain: did it sound right, was it said at the right time, was it correctly said, did it sound stupid? This was in English, yet the same thought processes pervaded, ruining any possible chance of being relaxed at any time. Also the brief moments when I felt more like myself were invalidated by my prolonged silences and introspectiveness.

My frustration at people not responding to what I said when so much effort was put in made me uncertain and was probably due to my paranoia: I believed that people took advantage of that, which infuriated me! I got fed up with hearing what I said corrected. I decided that if people weren't going to listen properly then I wasn't going to talk at all because every time I made the effort I was getting more and more hurt.

How ridiculous this sounds! It certainly doesn't sound like anything that the real Elaine would ever write! But nevertheless it was me who was reduced to that state. All this I did feel and, if I'm honest, do still, although I'm so ashamed of it all and ashamed of what I have become.

May I add here that I had to force myself not to change any of what I'd written but record the unabridged version!

With every condescending remark (as I saw it), I began to withdraw further and further. Just meeting and talking with people was humiliation itself because I felt I wasn't being treated or talked to as my intellect and my dignity required, but could find no way of stopping this from happening. I began to give up all hope of ever fitting in anywhere, of ever being special to anyone again or of ever being happy and settled anywhere. I slipped further into the darkness and confusion. My pride was deeply wounded, my dignity gone with a puff of wind and I began to question myself seriously only to find no integrity or individuality left, all I saw was emptiness. What's more, I realized only too well how inconsistent, confused and mixed-up I felt and how I portrayed myself to others, which made me feel humiliated and unworthy of anyone's individual attention.

I felt for a long time that I'd lost my place in the world, that I no longer mattered, that I no longer counted. The loss of face was unbearable and it was painful to see everybody going about confident, happy, balanced lives. I no longer had my identity, my confidence, an active life, a wide circle of friends or my independence. I did not feel that I belonged in the family – they seemed like strangers. I could no longer communicate with relatives, visitors.

I was infuriated by the family's lack of attention, acknowledgement and respect. They didn't seem to care about or even notice the distress signals I was sending out. This anger turned to pain and then to isolation as I cut myself off to prevent being hurt. In fact the feeling of isolation came back from Spain with me and has stayed ever since.

A deep sense of loss and regret pervaded my every thought, which turned into a deep sorrow. Casual remarks, condescensions to my (only recently realized) delicate, sensitive, vulnerable self were absorbed and added to the already mounting hurt and sense of total and utter hopelessness.

I felt lost, I felt like nothing, like a nobody. I had been cut down and struck off unfairly. Every environment was now hostile. My self-image was shattered along with my hopes, dreams and ambitions. Everything was crumbling before my eyes. I felt totally broken and torn apart. I felt I'd never amount to anything, that the rest of my life would be a painful, bitter struggle.

I write in the past tense because I find it easier. They are rather exaggerated, pitiful, incoherent thoughts and feelings that I have; the past tense distances them from myself because I'm ashamed that they were (and still are) mine. Neither am I in the habit of ruminating about every thought and feeling I have and expressing it on paper, but my desperation has caused me to compromise myself so much – to talk and act foolishly – that I did not feel foolish about writing all this down.

Apart from the incessant inner turmoil, through all the darkness there has been a spiritual struggle, which would be hard to put down on paper but is a small voice reminding me that I've become everything I dreaded becoming, that I'm a miserable failure, that God has deserted me. Sometimes this voice has been so audible it's been scary. I do know that the Devil is real and that he seeks the demise of all Christians, especially by preying on their weaknesses. I've become aware that my self-defeatist attitude and the darkness I've experienced has not been all my doing!

The night after making a real and desperate attempt to end all the strife, after leaning over the bath crying out from the depths of my soul, quite happily watching my blood spattering down the sides of the bath I know that the Devil was probably rubbing his hands in glee! I still find I can afford a litle bit of sarcasm to prove that although mixed up and confused my sanity is still quite intact!

Another brief note jotted down in response to what somebody said instead of trying to argue it all out.

I've tried everything over the past year and a half to sort things out, to make things better. I've tried every tactic I could think of, analysed the personalities of people I know, analysed every situation, torn myself to pieces, only to see things get worse and worse. It's like every time things get a bit better, I'm thrown against this brick wall and I'm too covered in 'bruises' to want to try again. When I say I've given up, I mean it. I'm too scared to give of myself any more and I just don't know who to be or how to be it and I feel too empty, drained and burnt out to even want to try.

After three suicide attempts, I realized that I really didn't like myself any more (to say the least). I want to be anybody else but me! I would not say that my initial problem was a poor self-image, but my fall to disgrace, as I see it, is real and the desolation, the pain, the confusion and the humiliation of what I've become is real. Everything I've written has come from deep within me. Suffering (like I never would have believed possible) was not exactly what I had lined up for my plan for life!

I have an underlying fear of the future, of failure, which rears its ugly head every time I try to do something constructive or positive. A small pessimistic voice that's always saying, Why bother? What's the point? Living seems to be all in the past, painfully existing in the present – and the future just seems too uncertain to think about. I fear that I may never hold my head high again and be a person in my own right. I hear all the advice about what I should do and the steps I should take. Sometimes I feel even more hopeless when I hear this, other times I feel like a bitter failure that's let everybody down and other times I just don't listen because it's the very obvious advice that I'm only too aware of myself but just don't seem to have the willpower or even the desire to put into action. When I see the love and concern people have recently been displaying, I feel very guilty. I feel almost like a fake. Sometimes I feel like the spoilt child whose pride and stubborness will not allow her to step down from her self-created cloud nine and get on with the nitty-gritty grind of living without the good feelings or the security to help her. Will I always have to live my life in shame from now on? Am I too selfish, too proud? Am I basically just a rotten, horrible person who has to have things on her own terms or not at all? Now that I have no illusions or dreams left, what do I replace them with? Will I always have to accept a second-rate life?

The self-recriminations, the questions and the analysis of everything never stop. The utter frustration and desolation of what I've been feeling is indescribable. Sometimes I drive myself almost crazy by longing for my old self to come back. I have confused myself more and more and sometimes I fear I'm losing my mind!

The simple solution to this would be to stop thinking like this – about who to be – be myself and just get on with things. I feel like thumping people when I get this response.

Oh God, why has all this happened. What is the lesson I've to learn? Do you intend to strip me totally bare, expose all my shame, all my sinfulness and self-ishness before you allow me to live again? The sinking feeling that things will never be the same again is almost sickening. Oh, how I long for some peace and security! (And maybe a little success in my life for a change, if I have the nerve to ask for that as well!!)

To be honest, I have been loved all my life. I can't claim to have had an emotionally deprived, stormy childhood or any of the usual sad stories that cause infinite problems for people later in life. I was popular, happy, secure and generally quite liked myself. I could relate to absolutely everyone. I could express wise opinions and assess most situations and people from early on – it sounds a bit like the story of Job in the Old Testament! I was just me, me was good enough, none of these thoughts ever crossed my mind. I thought I was quite a strong person and never imagined I'd be prone to these sorts of emotional and identity problems. (I've obviously been sorely misled somewhere along the line.) It's all been extremely hard for me to accept – I've made things worse for myself because of this.

Why did everything fall apart when I came back from Spain? Was it because all the 'pillars' had been removed and I suddenly became aware of how fragile and vulnerable I was? Where do these feelings of suppression come from? Why do I feel so let down by people? Why is it suddenly everything I was living for is gone? (Probably not a very intelligent question – I probably never questioned things before, but accepted them as they were.) Why do I feel like I'm 19 going on 29 but somewhere deep inside there's a 13-year-old that was never allowed to develop properly? I'm not a pessimist by nature, in fact the reverse is probably true – why has everything become so negative and complex? I'm searching for an integrated maturity, adulthood; I'm searching to become something better because I've lost myself. I want to be somebody who is respected (and who has self-respect!), who is strong and mature.

Do I seek perfection when it's unattainable? If that's so, I'll probably always be disillusioned.

Why, when I'm aware that my own personal value to God is infinite, eternal and unchanging, can I not convince myself of my own personal value and worth? I feel like an empty 'me' that is isolated and emotionally cut off from others. I feel like 'me' that can't seem to relate to others – or won't for fear of being hurt or being made to look stupid or not valued enough. I feel like 'me' that knows I'm messed up and confused and hurt and doesn't like any of the changes that are happening.

Do I also seek to become a perfect Christian? I am seeking God's will for my life and essentially want to become what he wants me to become. I sought a special touch of divine love to heal all my doubts. It did not materialize.

Also, I should be believing that my loss is my gain!

A part of me has a terrible fear of being mocked, but, looking at my present situation, I think I have nothing to lose!

In an attempt to sort myself out I have revealed a lot about myself, me and my secrets are out in the open! I feel incredibly vulnerable.

I know I must set down some guidelines and find myself before I can carry on to be anything, although in my depression I have been incapable of making even the smallest decision.

Right now the only thing I'm sure of is that I feel like a disgraced fool who is also very scared and broken-hearted. I feel scared that I can't and won't relate to anybody and, even if I could, what on earth is there to say? I also feel scared by the depth of my emotions and thoughts. What a mess!

I won't and don't want to live life from this terribly insecure, empty, vulnerable stance, feeling totally useless and inadequate, powerless and unhappy. I won't be compromised to this point. At times I feel very, very angry, filled with rage at what's happened. It's taken me all this time to admit I had all these problems and at that very point and time I gave up. My will is completely broken! And I honestly don't think that any amount of psychiatric counselling will give me back what I've lost.

I feel I have no future left at all. I have looked for signs of improvement, but I have only seen the reverse happening. I seem to slip further and further each day. I don't know how much longer I can bear reality. All I can see is this painful self-perpetuating vicious circle. (At this point, when I was writing all this I can remember feeling so angry that I was ready to hit anybody who spoke to me!) There are times I feel so angry I could really do something destructive – considering the reason and the event that prompted me to write this note, I suppose I already have! But fortunately, or unfortunately, I did not succeed in achieving the aim of my destructiveness.

CHAPTER 4

'Hold the hand which moulds your pain'

It might be helpful at this point to say that there are organizations such as the National Schizophrenia Fellowship which help relatives of people who have mental health problems. Unfortunately, Stuart and I, like far too many parents, have had to find out all this information for ourselves. After the diagnosis in 1991, it took me six months before I could think about the word 'schizophrenia' in connection with my only daughter. And it took me much longer before I could seek help. For a start, I didn't know where to look. Also, I had no energy. As one father put it, coping with schizophrenia is totally energy sapping, but, over and above this, carers have to be support workers, research workers – and agitators for change as well.

I now understand that I needed help to seek help, and the purpose of this book is to share with you the paths I have been led along on my journey – a journey not across time and space, but into myself to find resources to cope with this illness. Just at the time when Elaine's schizophrenia was diagnosed, I had to have a hysterectomy. I had many months to prepare for this. Subjectively, the thing which helped me most was the season of the year: autumn. All about me, the trees were shedding their unwanted leaves and I began to educate myself towards shedding something of me which I certainly didn't need any more.

Objectively, it was helpful to have open discussions with the consultants concerned and to be fully informed about what was to happen to me. Also, as the months progressed, I felt less and less well. The contrast with my twin sister was striking. There she was, already a granny at 47, bounding along in town, doing her Christmas shopping, while I could hardly keep up with her.

And at home, we had our distressed daughter and no information, no education. Nothing.

Another thing which was very useful was a series of artwork and meditation classes I attended. Part of me scoffed, 'This is a self-indulgent exercise for people with time on their hands and money in their pockets.' I thought of my twin sister, who was doing a useful morning's work as a nurse out on the district, caring for people while I was sloshing paint on paper with both hands together, taking nuts and feathers and stones into my hands, moulding clay and listening to music.

Here's a short poem which came out of those Friday morning sessions.

Destiny

What is your destiny? The world.
What is your heritage?
Sunshine and rain.
Mould your sorrow, roll, hold.
Music plays. The earth, the year, the time's the same.
Love the earth which brings to birth,
hold the hand which moulds your pain.
A woman with a basket offers eggs,
painted, warm. Follow her. No words,
no end in sight, but the path is plain.

In fact, the path was not plain, as I agonized over my daughter's wasted life. Nor could I 'hold the hand which moulds your pain'. But, because the class was based on prayer and very gently and skilfully guided by someone who was in her own way a wounded healer, I reaped the benefits of these three hours of stillness and self-exploration.

I found no solutions at all to the pain of seeing my lovely daughter so wounded or living with the accusations she kept heaping on me. It was getting impossible for us both to be under one roof together. In fact, at that time someone said to me, 'The mother–daughter relationship is the closest one there is, and if you are wounded in that, you are wounded in all else.' This man was about to do some major wounding himself – by walking out on his marriage – but his words helped me greatly.

It's not just the mother–daughter relationship. We are created to relate and when we are wounded in a close relationship, then we are truncated and crippled in all aspects of living.

So, wounded as a mother, I went under the surgeon's knife. After the operation, as I looked at the young nurses, Elaine's age, bustling about the ward, manoeuvring patients and complicated machinery, I truly realized that what we had on our hands was not normal. That Elaine was sick.

The afternoon after my operation, when I was still strung up with tubes, Stuart came to see me. As usual, the focus of our discussion was Elaine. 'They're going to admit her to mental hospital. The GP has fixed it up. I'm taking her up later this afternoon by car.'

I lay there, thinking and praying as the afternoon wore on.

And can you imagine who appeared at my bed? Elaine herself!

'Hello, Mum.'

I'd hardly seen her in outdoor clothes for months, and here she was. 'She's done a bunk,' I worried. 'They've admitted her and she's run away.'

Now I look back, I wonder why I didn't ask her directly, but then there had been so little communication between us for so long. As it was, I spent a sleepless night after what is considered to be quite a major operation. I didn't think about myself, I worried about my daughter. I was convinced she was sleeping rough somewhere.

It was two days before I heard from Stuart what had happened.

They had driven together to the hospital, Elaine weeping all the way. It was late in the afternoon and no consultant was on duty. The young registrar on duty took one look at Elaine and refused to admit her. 'This is the looney bin,' this doctor said. 'It's not for people like you.' And she sent an anguished father and a relieved daughter away.

It took ten more days and a call from a neighbour to the GP, urging her to do *something*, before Elaine was finally admitted by the consultant, who was later to interview us and give us that stark diagnosis.

And no information whatsoever, even though it's well known that carers need to strike a delicate balance every day, 24 hours of the day, trying to create that impossible thing in family life: an atmosphere of no stress.

The contrast with general medicine is enormous. I was given a booklet in which every detail of my treatment was described. I paid heed to the instructions I was given, did all my exercises, tottered out for short walks – my twin sister took me up to stay with her in Aberdeen, away from the stress at home. And I made a quick and good recovery.

Yet, for a major mental illness like schizophrenia, there was only that one interview in a bare room – no leaflets, no literature, no information. And the hospital itself was filthy. It's had a bit of a clean up since, but the wards are bare and sad. Lost, even bizarre men and women drift around, making weird noises, weird gestures, screaming. Staff don't wear uniforms, but someone sits beside the door ready to intercept would-be runaways or deal with quarrels.

It's a grim, grim place. All right, it may be an improvement on the vast institutions of the past, where patients wore uniforms and were routinely beaten or confined in strait jackets, but it's a long way from the standards most of us expect from our health service. No wonder Elaine, and many, many others, recall psychiatric hospital with a shudder and fear being sent back there.

When we were children, my twin and I used to toast ourselves at the fire and play games based on the titles of the books on the shelves. A book called *Private Worlds* intrigued us, not because of its title but because of its author's surname. It was Bottom with an 'e'!

One day, I pulled it from the shelf and read it. I'm sure I understood very little of it because the 'private worlds' of the title was the world of the mentally ill.

That book and the shoddy, inhospitable rooms of the mental hospital inspired the following poem.

Parents' Books

They stood stolidly ranged beside hearth flames,
hard covers gathering fine coal dust.
Like family friends we knew their names;
writer and title were part of childhood games –
the baggage children take on trust.

You see them yet among chipped china, racks
of cast-off clothes, glossier paperbacks,
aged and staid, smelling of must.

One, I recall, opened up the taboo
and individual world of the mentally ill:
an odd book for a nine-year-old to choose!
Or, could it be, some hobgoblin
doomed me as a child to deal
with the fact and function of a hospital?

Where, off-loaded second hand in barren rooms,
to divert the minds of the distressed –
like family portraits in worn-out frames
are books our parents valued most.

In the last chapter I mentioned that, at one point, Elaine
lived in what is known as supported accommodation. For
a single person who suffers from schizophrenia this is
often the ideal solution. Supported accommodation is
linked with various housing associations that buy or build
properties. Sometimes they may be big houses, subdivided,
as in student bed-sits. There are shared kitchens, bathrooms
and sitting rooms, but each person has their own bedroom. Each house has a warden to see that the property
is maintained in working order and deal with practical
difficulties which arise, but not to be a counsellor.

Each person living in such a house is given a support
worker and there are regular house meetings. Shopping

and cooking meals are shared and there is a rota which has to be followed.

I have a friend who spent 14 years in a top-security hospital. When I got to know him he was enjoying the more open conditions of a normal psychiatric hospital, but was still kept under close supervision in a locked ward. Later he moved into supported accommodation, run by Penumbra, a voluntary organization. I shall write more about this later. The move improved his life dramatically. First he lived with others, but now, in his fifties, for the first time since student days, he has set up home in a pleasant, modern flat on his own.

No one suggested supported accommodation to us at first. Penumbra's Young Persons Project wasn't in existence when Elaine's illness was first diagnosed. Started in 1993, the Project now provides 142 places for young people aged between 16 and 23, offering a safe, stable environment, a halfway house between home and hospital. Support workers take the focus away from their clients' mental health problems and aim to help young people move safely into adult life. The classic 'revolving door' syndrome of constant readmission to hospital is noticeably reduced.

But none of this was available to us. Stuart and I had already decided that our next step together was to move to Russia. We packed our possessions. Elaine lay in bed, not taking medication, not participating in life. It began to look as if the removers would be carrying her out in her bed.

However, while I was packing around her, I came across a diary. She'd written it the year before, as her world was crumbling. At one point, a youth worker tried to involve Elaine as a helper on her project, thinking that this might improve Elaine's self-esteem. Elaine wrote about this – she let me read it as I sat on the floor beside her bed, sorting through her things. I found that diary immensely illuminating. Elaine described sitting in a minibus with the teenagers she was supposed to be befriending and feeling as if there were an invisible barrier between herself and them.

I later read that this is quite typical. People can feel cut off from those they love as if by some impenetrable wall of plate glass – you can see through it, but cannot reach out to others on the other side.

You might wonder why Stuart and I were callous enough to go to Russia and leave our sick daughter behind – and there were those who voiced that sentiment, mostly behind our backs.

We had made our first moves before we realized there was a serious mental health problem in our family, but other family members, close friends like Carol and her family, people in the church who had held on to Elaine through her bad times were all unanimous. Elaine will do better without you around, they all said.

In fact, as with everything, a compromise situation is truer. Some family support is helpful, but there should be other structures too – the much-vaunted 'care in the community', which has such a hollow sound.

However, as we worried over what housing provision we could make for Elaine, we heard that a girl from another church, a nurse, wanted a flatmate right in the heart of the area where many of our own church families live. So Elaine moved there, but before she did, because she was so withdrawn and had been without medication for so long, I begged the psychiatrist to readmit her to hospital.

'We'll go for a Section 24', she said. This jargon was becoming familiar to us. Under the Mental Health (Scotland) 1984 Act, there are three sections which are commonly used to make sure that a person receives in-patient treatment. Section 24 is used most often in an emergency. A person is detained in hospital for 72 hours, giving the doctors a chance to review the situation. Elaine's doctor thought that she would extend this Section to a further 28-day period, a Section 26, and she actually phoned us from her own home at 8.30 a.m. to tell us that this is what she was going to do.

Stuart went up to visit Elaine in hospital and found that, once again, the system had failed us. Elaine had been discharged.

We left for a six-week period in St Petersburg with heavy hearts and learnt from phone calls home that our worst fears were justified. The girl with whom Elaine was supposed to be sharing had an accident and was admitted to hospital for the full six weeks of our time away. Elaine became more ill than we have ever known her. She became more and more oblivious to the world around her, no longer lying in bed but sitting alone in an unheated room, seemingly indifferent to her own physical needs. She wasn't able to cook for herself, she could barely even eat. She would leave the flat and walk. Where to? Nowhere. Just walk, up and down the stairs, up and down the pavement outside – her boots were worn with all the walking. And now we experienced the community's hatred and fear. Neighbours called the police. One person made hate phone calls to us and anyone connected with us.

We touched down from Russia to be immediately taken up with Elaine's problems and needs – and this is a continuing scenario.

I phoned the hospital. 'Look, it's dreadful, you've got to do something.'

'We'll go for the jugular', the doctor said.

By that he meant: the dreaded Section 18. It is applied where 'patients' symptoms are longstanding and they have refused treatment and/or in-patient care for some months'. The Section must be approved by a sheriff court. It can be applied for up to six months and can be renewed thereafter. Patients are admitted to hospital without their consent, but they do have a right of appeal.

I understand that the legislation is changing and Elaine is likely to be placed on a Care in the Community Order when her present Section expires. In other words, instead of being described as on 'leave of absence' from hospital, as she is at the moment, she will be on an order requiring her to receive treatment if she wishes to remain in the community, and she should be given a 'package of care' tailored to her needs.

That December, unable to live alone, Elaine came back to live with us. A friend lent us a car and I drove her up to see the doctor. She walked out of the interview in disgust. I understood that he would set the procedures in motion straight away. He delayed and Christmas intervened and so nothing was done.

While we were waiting for something to happen to help our daughter, Stuart and I spoke at a church meeting about our work in Russia. At least, Stuart spoke about Russia. I poured out my sorrows about Elaine. A man drew me to one side. 'There's an article in *The Telegraph* today about schizophrenia,' he said. 'It highlights the work of an organization called SANE.'

Later that day, the article plopped through the letter-box. What great kindness – to go out of his way to deliver the article, and then not intrude any further! People who act in hidden ways are truly sensitive.

The article was about a new telephone link called SANEline which would operate much as the Samaritans do. SANE stands for Schizophrenia, a National Emergency. The patron of this voluntary organization is the Prince of Wales. SANE was set up after a series of articles in *The Sunday Times* in 1989 by a journalist called Marjorie Wallace who was awarded the Journalist of the Year Award for her work. She became aware of the hidden misery of schizophrenia, which is the cause of one in ten of all suicides in this country. She saw the anguish of families, some of whom are 'held hostages in their own homes, living in fear of what their distressed sons and daughters may do'. She saw the desperate plight of parents who, like Stuart and myself, were torn by trying to meet the needs of our sick daughter only to be told by the professionals that we were 'colluding with her illness'. From that article we discovered we weren't the only parents who were made to feel inept nuisances when we sought help. My computer is overloaded with letters I have written to GPs and psychiatrists about Elaine's isolation, inertia, lack of medication. I have only ever had one reply to any one of these letters, and it basically told me to mind my own business. No professional has set any guidelines for us to follow, even though Elaine's well-being depends on the right sort of environment.

Now, here at last, in the black and white print of the newspaper was a description of families like ours, and the information that a telephone helpline was going to be set up. Later that year, I was to use that helpline. It took me a long time to get through. I spoke to someone called John. I said, 'What's the use of having a helpline if you can't get through?' John said, 'I know. I'm sorry. We're inundated with calls and we're all volunteers. I've just come on duty.'

John listened patiently while I poured out my sorrows and then he said, and I've never forgotten it, 'You've been telling me about your daughter. What about *you*?' It's vitally important for carers to make space for themselves, to consider their own needs.

But that was in the future. That December, we were waiting daily for Elaine to be admitted to hospital. We were tired after six weeks on a hard bed settee in Russia. We were preparing to go back in January and then Elaine's only home would be her bed in the mental hospital, where, we had been told, she would spend at least three months as an in-patient.

However, we knew that when she got a weekend or overnight pass – or if she 'did a runner' – she had somewhere to go. She would be welcomed by her friend Carol, her husband Paul and their three daughters. They have held on to Elaine all through the years of her illness. She has gone on holiday with them and has been made to feel truly part of their family.

Elaine wasn't admitted to hospital until the middle of January, literally on the eve of our return to Russia. We went through all the procedures. Her psychiatrist visited our home. Her GP called. Social workers, mental health officers visited – and so did two men in black ties who came from the court with a notice that Elaine threw down with fine disdain.

That evening, Stuart went off on his bike to pray with a group of people who support us in our work in Russia. Elaine went to bed at 7 p.m. I sat on the floor of our front room and struggled with Russian grammar. We had been given the use of a beautiful Georgian flat in Edinburgh's lovely New Town, but those big rooms take some heating and it was freezing. I huddled as close as I could to the gas fire.

At about 9.30, I felt an impulse to go through to the kitchen. I remember thinking, 'What am I doing this for? Is it to put the kettle on? But I don't want a cup of tea.'

Sitting on a chair in the small living room off the kitchen was Elaine. She was wearing a short nightshirt. Her arms, legs and feet were bare, but she seemed oblivious of the cold. Her gaze was focused on the object she held in her right hand – the bread knife, serrated on both sides and with a pronged end.

'Elaine,' I said, 'give me that knife.'

Her grip on the handle tightened.

I said, 'Well, let me make you a cup of coffee.'

I switched on the kettle. She was not in my line of vision any more. I turned back towards her with the coffee and saw that the colour had faded out of her face. She had turned chalk-white.

'Elaine,' I said, 'you've taken something, haven't you. Tell me. What have you taken?'

That month Elaine had hardly spoken. She often made little noises in her throat and later she told me that she thought she was talking. So she didn't answer me, but she turned her wrist towards me. Blood was welling out of the cut she had made.

But she relinquished the knife.

I gave her the coffee and raced to phone the psychiatric hospital. I felt that someone so desperate should surely be given help straight away, but there was no way she could be admitted until the next day. 'Phone 999' I was advised.

The ambulance arrived. Elaine's wrist was only superficially wounded. It was soon bandaged up. She refused to go to casualty and, indeed, there was no need. She took herself off to bed. The woman in the team went along to her room to talk to her while the man stayed and talked to me. I showed him a painting Elaine had done which hung over our sideboard.

The ambulance woman came back. 'She won't talk to me', she said.

'She won't talk to anyone,' I told her, not for the first time. 'She should be in hospital. She needs help.'

The ambulance crew left. I ransacked the house for every sharp instrument I could find and hid knives, scissors, a pizza cutter and so on. Stuart came home. 'We were praying for you', he said. Was it their prayers which had driven me into the kitchen that evening? Some inner urging had made me go.

'I'm not going to bed tonight,' I told him. 'How can we sleep? I've hidden all the knives but she might do something else.'

But we slept just the same, and next day I ordered a taxi and took her to hospital. I have seen mental patients dragged along the ground by the police in an attempt to get them into an ambulance and I wanted to spare my daughter that indignity.

Can you guess what I found in her room when I got back home from the hospital? Elaine's bed was in our second bedroom which doubled as Stuart's study. And because half our stuff was in boxes, some was in Russia and the rest was about to be packed, we had some odd things lying around.

Including an axe.

A blunt axe, I grant you, but still, an axe.

Elaine went very unwillingly to hospital, but she stayed in and was given medication. Up until now she has always responded very quickly to the medication and so, although she was still far from well, she began to be aware of the world around her – aware, too, that her father and I were returning to Russia and that she would have nowhere to live. And so she ran away.

We had a dramatic motor bike chase across town. Elaine was brought back to our flat on the back of her brother's bike. Her long raincoat was in shreds. It had caught in the spokes of the wheel. She could have been dragged off the bike and seriously injured. An ambulance called at our flat. Elaine was in tears, but, in the end, she agreed to go back to hospital. The next day I went to visit. I found that Elaine had been weeping for over two hours. She had tried to run away again and was threatened with being put into a locked ward.

I was distressed for Elaine and furious with the hospital. What is the sense of going through all this fraught business of court orders, having all these professionals come into our home, for the hospital then not to be able to contain our daughter?

We left for Russia next day.

Here is Elaine's comment on the experience.

I first went into hospital because I read my Bible and there it was assumed that I had an illness of sorts. I had various unpleasant experiences with the people in there and was always very guarded against them. Friends were appalled at the fact that I was in there. However, I believed that I had a covenant of health with God that is sacred and binding. This was not refuted initially.

Then in 1991, I moved back with my parents and all of a sudden I found myself under a Sheriff's Court Order. I still don't understand why I was forcibly removed from my home and into hospital where I was allowed a degree of freedom and escaped at the weekends whenever possible. . . .

I was forced to take injections. I was treated very badly, whereby the doctors refuted various aspects of my religion and generally usurped the role of my parents. However, God spoke to me during that time and assured me that I was in the right, that I was suffering wrongs unjustly.

On my release I suffered badly from the effects of

institutionalization. The whole experience put me through so much pain and injustice that indeed I should not have experienced. I was very surprised to find out that it was thought that I was still ill and that a Section 18 should be renewed. I appealed against this decision but it was refuted.

I found it ridiculous that at 22 I was being treated like a child when my parents had released to me the authority of being a free agent, an adult in my own right. To my utter surprise I found that the Section was being renewed once more purely to force me to take medication when I considered myself to be well and healthy. On various occasions I fought with nurses, arguing out the fact that I did not want to take medication, as indeed it has always been against my principles and I have disliked the idea. As a Christian we should genuinely question medical science, especially when it involves ethical issues and the use of drugs or foreign substances to our body.

This is a God-given right which was overruled time and time again. The normal state of the human body is one of health. I resented the assumption that this was not the case with me.

Can you imagine anything worse than being incarcerated in a miserable hospital when you genuinely do not understand that there is anything the matter with you, when the injections you are forced to take make you feel awful and when, as in Elaine's case, you believe that to take medication is to limit the healing power of God?

As for myself, I was as far away as ever from finding a solution to my anguish. Perhaps as a way of learning to 'hold the hand which moulds my pain', I started a little notebook called 'The Goodness of God'. I noted a text from my Russian Bible, from Psalm 92: 'The Lord is just;

there is no injustice within him.' And underneath I added the words of Jesus: 'You do not realize now what I am doing, but later you will understand.'

My poems are one way in which I struggle to 'understand' and so I'd like to end this chapter with three brief poems which grope for comfort in the face of the 'haunted wilderness' of my daughter's life and that hackneyed metaphor, community care.

Care Plans

In the Community

Officers – on paper – are in place
but fail to pass
the haunted wilderness
where a young woman chainsmokes
locked in inner space.
Unopened mail floods her untrod floor –
and I am pinioned on a hackneyed metaphor.

Breakdown

Once, conversation was a good ordering of
    possibilities;
the commonplace pulsed with melodious sounds.
Now words are stones;
I find no hospice for my wounds.

There's a story in the Gospels about a foreign woman who begged Jesus to heal her daughter, saying that, even as an outsider, a non-Jew, she had a right to eat the crumbs which fell from the table. I, too, am a mother crying out for help for my daughter, and as I seek those 'crumbs of comfort' I find that, paradoxically, sorrow is its own remedy.

Remedy

Comfort may seem spare,
but crumbs are not denied the poor.

The store of the destitute – of necessity – is bare.

For where there is no voice, no one is dumb;
where there is no choice, less may equal some.

Out of the destitution and need of Russia, out of the
destitution of my heart touched by the blessing of sorrow,
out of the impoverishment of schizophrenia, I continued
to seek the goodness of God, whose hand moulds mercy
as well as pain.

CHAPTER 5

'Talitha koum'

House Facing Winter

Choosing the sunshine, I try to forget
she's in the shadows, sleeping at noon-time;
try to find comfort in birdsong, waken each
    morning
to cadences carolled from branches and bushes
    around me,
while she is shuttered in her summer of stupor,
a full-blown June rose, beautiful, blighted,
living with me in this house facing winter:
for the sun doesn't brighten our windows,
    visit our garden.

Poems can paint pictures as a camera captures a scene on film. That short poem was a snapshot, in words, of a walled garden. Blackbirds were shouting all around me – a sound we can capture in words but not on film – and, as the poem says, I was trying to 'choose the sunshine', but our house was still 'facing winter', because that's what schizophrenia is, and so that poem is about schizophrenia, too.

All relatives and close friends feel this onset of winter in their family lives. Everyone finds it hard to cope. The family member who suffers from schizophrenia is so sensitive, indeed fragile, that they often interpret even the best-intentioned remark wrongly. Medication helps some of the symptoms, but not all. Those last months on medication under the Section 18 had brought Elaine back to reality, but she still had little insight into her needs. And she still, as in the poem, spent a lot of the day in bed.

She was waiting for a place in supported accommodation, and it took three months after her discharge from hospital before a room became available. Stuart was in Russia and I, because of Elaine's needs, had stayed at home for the summer of 1992. We were privileged to still be allowed the use of the flat in Edinburgh's historic New Town from which Elaine had been admitted to hospital in January 1992.

The flat was north-facing, but, apart from the lack of sun, I loved being there – a quiet corner in the centre of a lovely city. I set up my computer, did mental gymnastics with my Russian grammar and tried not to focus on Elaine. I wasn't successful. Elaine's dependence, her helplessness and the many, many hours she spent in bed each day had me climbing the walls. It had gone on for four years now – the best years of her life spent in a wilderness place. One day I reached a crisis.

I was an eyewitness to an accident. I'd gone out to post a letter to Stuart just after 9 o'clock. Doors opened. Elderly ladies, each one seemingly older than the next, appeared at Georgian doorways with little dogs on leads. I conjectured their lives within these gracious flats. And the statistic came like a horrible mantra: 1 in 100 worldwide, schizophrenia affects 1 in 100.

Take 100 doors in the street. Would I find someone who had schizophrenia behind one of them?

The unanswerable questions hammered at me: 'Why us? Why our lovely daughter?'

I walked on in tears while the life of the city flowed

around me. Brakes screeched. A van skidded to a halt. I turned and saw a woman being catapulted through the air. She landed on the back of her head in the road. Her yellow shopping bag went flying ahead. There was a trickle of blood, a wetness when they finally lifted her.

That life cut off, ended so terribly, made me think of Calvary – that public lonely violent death – of the millions and millions of deaths of the Holocaust, of my own incurable pain. I felt numb, paralysed. Somehow I got myself to the post office. People were discussing the accident. I had to fight with myself not to cry. When I got home, Elaine was still in bed. I knew, rationally, I couldn't expect her to support me, but I was turned to stone.

Mist swirled around me, a typical Edinburgh haar. The rest of the country was enjoying a heatwave. Indeed, we'd hardly seen the sun all week. It was so cold I couldn't get the washing dry. I had to use gas fires and even central heating in this north-facing Edinburgh house while the rest of the country sweltered.

The house of my spirit was cold, too. I had watched my beautiful daughter become withdrawn, hostile and stop functioning. I had seen her admitted to mental hospital, come out doped to the eyeballs so that people ask if she's fey. I had seen her take herself off medication and retreat into a world so private that she smoked matches instead of cigarettes, made sounds in her throat instead of speech, so that she was finally dragged off to hospital and confined against her will

She was now injected with heavy medication, which masks but does not cure her symptoms, and has unpleasant side-effects. She was struggling in vain to get jobs or start courses where they ask 'What is your general health?' This total blank on her c.v. has been caused by an illness she doesn't perceive she suffers.

As I was saying, she was about to be housed in supported accommodation. Her flatmates would be young people with problems, social as well as medical.

I knew by now that I should let well alone, switch off Elaine and her problems, but it's hard when you're mother and daughter sharing a flat. My spirit was grieving over this wasted young life, not realizing its potential.

When you walk this knife edge, you learn to be thankful for small mercies. As the poem which ended the last chapter reminds us, 'The store of the destitute – of necessity – is bare.'

Out of this barren store I continued to search for comfort. Emotional exhaustion had dragged me right down. A friend sent a card and the tender message inside seemed to come from another world, a place I knew once, but was no longer part of. I gave the card pride of place on the windowsill. These small actions can almost be a prayer.

I added the words on the card to prayers I treasure, the Kyries from the Coronation Mass of King James V. I wrote the words into my prayer book. These beautiful praises could pray when I could not.

Lord, King, resplendent in heaven, have mercy on your people: the hosts of cherubim hymn you perpetually and proclaim with praise unceasing, have mercy on us.

Christ, King, high-throned, the angels praise you with beautiful songs, have mercy.

Christ, whom the church praises throughout all the world, whom the sun, moon and stars, earth and sea serve forever, have mercy.

Dearest child of the blessed Virgin Mary, redeemer of those you have purchased from the power of death with your own blood, upon this your flock, have mercy.

Sun of the most shining splendour, arbiter of justice, when you come to judge all nations strictly, we beseech you have mercy.

The choir also sang the same composer's setting of a Prayer to my Most Holy Jesus.

O good Jesus, most loving Jesus, have mercy on me. O most forgiving Jesus, by that precious blood which you shed for sinners, look favourably on me, wretched and unworthy. O Jesus, beloved, delightful, examine what is yours in me and remove what is alien. O, most beloved Jesus, O most longed for Jesus, O most gentle Jesus, allow me to enter your kingdom.

I particularly held on to the words '. . . remove what is alien', not only because it's a little pun on Elaine's name and I'm sure the Lord enjoys word-play, but also because of the alien thoughts which have invaded her mind.

The Jesus prayer is an important part of Russian Orthodox prayer. I added two prayers from the Lenten liturgy.

As the Prodigal Son I come to you, Father. I have scattered the wealth you gave me. Take pity on me, cleanse me and clothe me again with the robe of your Kingdom.

I have transgressed more than the adultress, yet in no wise do I bring you floods of tears. Yet in silent prayer I fall down before you and with love embrace your most pure feet.

Prayer during those cold summer months of 1992 mostly took the form of cries of despair. I really was very blocked with pain, and when a friend wrote from Russia that Stuart and I have filled their home with optimism and hope – well!

The night of the car accident, I sat on the floor, partially cooked by the gas fire, and turned to a simple little book whose depths I shall never plumb, *Getting to Know You* by Etta Gullick (Mayhew-McCrimmoms, 1987). And here's what went through my head as I read.

Etta: Jacob wrestling with the angel was wounded....

Me: I am totally wounded – and everything else is blotted out.

Etta: The angel goes away without telling his name....

Me: Seems a bit of a cop out, just what we've grown to expect – like the Rabbis in Auschwitz who put God in the dock. It was Sunday, the Christian day of rest – they were required to work on the Jewish Sabbath, of course. And towards evening they held a trial: they were the jury, the accused was God. And they concluded: God is guilty, now, gentlemen, it's time for evening prayer.

Etta: God is not to be held on to and known as we would like him to be; rather **through being in our own situation he lets us know something more about ourselves and helps us with our problems but not in the way we want or expect** ...

Me: Not in the way we want or expect.... Then, how? I want my daughter to be made whole. But, wait a minute: 'he let's us know some thing more about ourselves' – this is getting closer. In other words, get me whole and I might be able to help Elaine. But I'm abrasive and nasty; I no longer welcome people. I'm dried up.

Then I remembered that the card I'd received had said something about me being loved by God and by others. I went through to the living room and reread the words: 'You are precious to God and to many of us. . .'. I wrote, 'I don't feel precious.' But Etta Gullick has an answer here and I copied it down: 'We have to withstand the pressures of ever-threatening despair and **let things be as they are. . . . It is not easy for us to accept as reality that God does love us whatever we are and whatever we are doing. We need great faith to accept God in the way in which he gives himself to us.'**

You bet we do, if he's trying to give himself to us through the illness of someone we love!

Isn't that what 'hold the hand which moulds your pain' means? Anyway, I decided to try to 'let things be as they are' and stop focusing on Elaine – just be glad that we're still together. I knew further steps must follow, but that was enough for one night.

When Elaine was six, she said to me, 'There are no Bible stories for girls, Mummy.'

I hastened to reply, 'Oh, but there's Rebecca, and Rachel, and Esther, and what about Mary and the angel?' And, of course, not just for but about a young girl – there's the story of the Raising of Jairus' Daughter.

Here's a snapshot of the story. Jairus, a wealthy and respected pillar of the synagogue, comes to Jesus with a desperate plea for help. And so desperate is he that he prostrates himself in the dust before the travel-stained young rabbi from Galilee. His 12-year-old daughter is at the point of death and Jairus begs Jesus to heal her.

Jesus goes with him at once. Jairus' relief is so great that no way is he going to stop to enquire whether the young rabbi is ritually cleansed, nor whether he has been defiled by recent contact with an outcast.

In fact, Jesus has been in close contact with an outcast

– a man who lived among the tombs, in a place of death, crying aloud and cutting himself. Jesus heals him and he sits 'clothed and in his right mind' at Jesus' feet.

I wonder where they got the clothes from in that desolate graveyard? I like to think it was Jesus' own cloak which the man was wearing (the one he had rolled up for a pillow in the storm-tossed boat the night before).

Anyway, off they go, the well-dressed leader of the synagogue and the rabbi and his rough and ready gang of followers.

The trouble is that Jesus, like the Princess of Wales, attracts the crowds. They jostle around, hemming in Jesus and Jairus, who are in such a desperate hurry. And in that mêlée, Jesus stops and asks, 'Who's touched me?'

There was at least one other desperate person in the crowd, a woman. She isn't wealthy or important. In fact, she's a complete outcast for, under the strict Law, upheld by Jairus, this woman, because of her medical complaint, defiled everything she touched. She was, in fact, as good as dead, and had been for 12 years.

The woman hasn't come publicly to Jesus. She doesn't dare speak to him. But she knows exactly what she must do. She reaches out and touches, not Jesus, but his clothing. One touch, she must have thought, will wipe away 12 years of misery. And so, secretly, she touches Jesus' clothes. She is healed immediately and only two people in all that crowd know what has happened: Jesus and the woman. Instead of pressing forward on his errand of mercy, Jesus stops and asks, 'Who touched me?'

Poor Jairus, whose need is so desperate, has to give way to an unclean woman. How vexed the disciples must have been! Wealthy, influential Jairus has abased himself publicly in front of their teacher and here Jesus is, making a complete fool of himself asking who touched him.

As for Jairus himself, he must have been nearly out of his mind with worry. He'd gone to such lengths to try to save his only daughter. It hadn't even seemed too much to throw himself down to the ground in front of Jesus. Perhaps, deep down, he wasn't too surprised that Jesus had agreed to help his child. Jairus is an important man. He's doing the young rabbi quite a favour by asking for his help and now, when every moment counts, everything is going wrong.

But Jesus knows what he is doing. He has to let the woman who touched him know for sure that she is really free and so he keeps on asking until he compels the woman whose furtive touch has sapped the strength of her healer to declare publicly what she has done. Perhaps because she can see how drained and exhausted Jesus now looks, she has the courage to stand in front of the crowd. She doesn't speak, but she falls trembling at his feet.

Jesus speaks directly to her. 'My daughter,' he says, 'your faith has made you well.'

So, she is restored to health. But, more than that, she has been restored to God's family. Jesus has said so, publicly praising her faith, calling her that lovely word, daughter. But even while Jesus is wasting everyone's time with this insignificant, unnamed woman (yet she has a name now, 'daughter') the news is broken to Jairus. 'Your daughter is dead. There's no need to bother the teacher any more.'

Before Jairus can make any sort of decision, Jesus turns to him. 'Don't be afraid, only have faith!'

Oh, Jesus, what are you expecting from this distraught father? *Only* have faith. Is it so easy, then? I pray. I try to do things right, but everything goes wrong. Instead of getting better, all my worst fears are realized. In fact, things beyond my worst imaginings. I have prayed so much for Elaine. I have reached the point over and over again where I have cried out, 'I can't stand it any more!' You wait there calmly saying, 'Don't be afraid, only have faith.'

And even when they get to Jairus' house and hear all the weeping and wailing, Jesus seems unperturbed. 'What's all the noise for? The wee one's not dead, but sleeping.'

The hired mourners laugh this nutcase to scorn. But Jesus is speaking with the simplicity of true faith. It will lead him to a garden, to judgement and to death. The simplicity of Jesus will crucify him.

The simplicity of Jesus will also stir the motionless body of the 12-year-old girl.

Once all the commotion of the hired mourners is over and done with, Jesus, alone in the room with the girl's grief-stricken parents and his three closest helpers, goes up to the dead child and takes her hand in his.

Peter, James and John look on amazed. Will Jesus really order the death he calls sleep to leave the child alone, just as, only yesterday he had commanded countless demons to stop tormenting the poor, naked man among the tombs? Would the voice that also only yesterday had scolded the wind and calmed the waves thunder forth and call life back into the child?

The words of Jesus are recorded in his own language – 'Talitha koum'.

These are not the words of power which might frighten the sleeping child, but tender, everyday, family words: the words of a big brother in Nazareth who wakens his small sister still curled on her sleeping mat when the first light of day shines across the flat rooves of the houses and chickens and children and goats tumble outside.

'Talitha, little girl, koum, it's time to get up.' And the girl opens her eyes and gets up at once.

Jesus, who made the frightened woman admit in front of a huge crowd that she had, indeed, touched him, now warns the girl's parents not to tell anyone what has happened. A child brought back from death is a wonder to hit the world's headlines. A little sister roused from sleep is an everyday occurrence. From the days of Moses on, we've expected God to work in stupendous ways – the stuff of the Hollywood epic, the parting of the sea, water from a rock, dry bones being miraculously filled with life. But Jesus makes a celebration of normal, everyday things, the commonplace events of daily life. A sower scattering seed, children squabbling, wild flowers become poems and stories; miracles are made of jars of well water, fish and wine and bread. And so he simply tells the parents to give their daughter something to eat, for the child needs her breakfast after such a long, deep sleep.

I have a picture of Christ the good shepherd and I often beg, please help my little sheep. You healed Jairus' daughter, why not step into our home and bring my girl back to life?

Some people paint out their pain. I reach for a pen. I use those words of Jesus, spoken in his own Aramaic language, 'Talitha koum', in a poem to Elaine, and with it I shall close this chapter. The other quotations in the poem come from Gerard Manley Hopkins, whose sonnet I mentioned in Chapter 2, and also from Shakespeare's play *Hamlet* with its beautiful, sad portrayal of Ophelia's madness. Shakespeare portrays a young person's schizophrenic breakdown with textbook accuracy, although the name 'schizophrenia' wasn't coined until 1911. The title of my poem comes from one of Ophelia's disjointed images – word association leaping into jumbled thought is very typical of schizophrenia.

The Owl is a Baker's Daughter . . .

The mind, mind has mountains. . .
the self-caves.
You felt your pit-props slip;
and we only knew we'd lost you
into a twilit existence,
entombed in a bedroom grave.

Life has pricked you sore,
your mind's fingers bleed,

Briar Rose, bewitched princess . . .

Once you ran
over sunlit shores, sang
to seals, swam,
turned cartwheels across the sand

It was Eden, then.
Your fair hair shone in the westering sun;
we knew nothing of the night to come:
did not fear the snake.

The roses of your womanhood
are eaten with this blight; the garden
you once tended is overgrown with weeds

the music you danced to, the songs,
the friends you used to phone
all turned off, in this long

unfriendly silence.
No rosemary for remembrance;
no heart's ease – only rue.
The owl is a baker's daughter.
can young girl's wits be mortal?

'Talitha koum'

I cast for comfort I can no more get,
never now see your blond head
among the crowds in Princes Street

among the crowds in Princes Street
are folk in wheelchairs; guys who sit
with placards, begging a meal, a bed,

but your boots no longer stride, your head
tosses on your pillows, haar or sun or wet
I cast for comfort . . . can no more get.

You wept:
we listened to a litany of loss
day and night, night and day:
'No one can feel
what's happened to me. This is for real . . .'.

When you were small
I carried you over cliffs,
laid you in a hollow,
that the earth might be your cradle,
April sun hold you;
you lay content,
eyes like quiet stars.

Talitha, koum . . .
I give you this rune:
larksong restore you,
warmth enfold you,
love blossom again.

Loss and Language, Chapman Publishing, Edinburgh, 1994

CHAPTER 6

'Discovering the hidden in the everyday'

In those grey summer months of 1992, when Elaine was staying with me in our 'house facing winter', I made another breakthrough.

I was aware of the existence of the National Schizophrenia Fellowship. I knew roughly where its office was, but I simply hadn't the energy or will to go and find out about it.

Just after the street accident I referred to in the last chapter, which drove me to batter at the gates of heaven for some response, and found me journeying into myself instead, I set off to look for the National Schizophrenia Fellowship.

We see people walking about the streets of our cities. We never know the internal dramas of their lives. No snapshot of me that bleak day in mid-May would have let a viewer guess that they were witnessing a woman who was setting out on a path she had long viewed with trepidation. I was going to have to take the dreaded name 'schizophrenia' and acknowledge it fully.

You see, we'd never been able to do this properly. We kept hoping for improvement, stability, some sort of return to normal life. Not long before the diagnosis was made in 1991, Elaine was in the front room with a friend from church who kept her doors open for our daughter and went to the trouble of coming to visit her in her fragile space. I heard them laughing and talking, and how glad I was for something which seemed like normal life!

Then Stuart came home. Here's a snapshot of my husband, cruising home on his racer bike, sweeping in towards the kerb. He wears a skid lid-style crash helmet, but, alas, the open bits expose his bald head! On that particular day he had just cycled 15 miles uphill, 15 miles back. He wheeled his bike through the front door to prop it in its usual place. You've guessed it, in the hall beside the radiator, just ready to catch against the washing and make it oily. I saw that his eyes were red. 'What's the matter, Stuart? Have you been crying? Is it the wind?' I asked.

He had been out at the Community of the Transfiguration whose brothers live in garden huts. Their lifestyle is akin to the hermit monks of Russia. There are only two brothers now, Roland and John, and Sister Patty has her own hut in a small mining town nearby. 'Bumbling,' Roland, aged 80, says, his apple-red cheeks creasing with mischievous laughter. 'Bumbling, that's what I do. I bumble.' Bumbling means you gear down, spend time in ways which won't get reflected in your pay cheque, discover the beauty of small, everyday things.

But Stuart's face put all my thoughts of bumbling away. 'Elaine has schizophrenia,' he told me. 'Roland's brother has it. He described the symptoms. They're the same as Elaine's.'

'Oh, but Stuart, she can't have,' I maintained. 'Things are fraught, I know, but she's laughing and talking, listen. People with schizophrenia are too withdrawn to do that.'

Now, in summer 1992, I was intent on brushing away all denial, of overcoming my most deep-seated fears and actively seeking help, however little I wanted to put myself or my daughter under the name 'schizophrenia'. I was passing a new milestone, but not one which would have shown up on any film: a milestone of the heart.

Milestones mark the places the road leads to and the distances we have to go. They don't tell us whether the route lies across rough ground or easy, nor how long it will take us to travel, but the important thing is that we know the name of our destination.

In her essays on the love of God, *Waiting on God* (Fount, 1994), Simone Weil writes that it was said that the Holy Grail would be given to the knight who knew the right question to ask of a king half-paralysed from a grievous wound. The question was a very simple one, but often the most obvious things are the ones we arrive at last. The question was this: 'What are you going through?'

That question invites someone who is suffering to share their experience from their point of view. They are invited to name the thing which hurts them most, just as I was going to have to pronounce the word 'schizophrenia'.

In this context I find the fairy story of Rumplestiltskin helpful. A miller boasted that his daughter could spin straw into gold. Not surprisingly, the King took her into his palace. He would marry her to his eldest son and all his kingdom would be hers if she could spin a roomful of hay into gold.

The poor girl sat and wept, but a helpful little goblin appeared and spun the straw for her. Gradually he became like an addiction, an obsession in her life. He told her he would carry her off with him to his den. She could only free herself if she found out his name. Soldiers were despatched far and wide throughout the kingdom and, in the end, one of them returned with the vital information. So when the goblin appeared, convinced that the girl and her kingdom were his, she gained the upper hand by telling him his name. The goblin disappeared in a rage and was never heard of again.

I was trying to win the upper hand and regain a measure of control over my attitudes to schizophrenia.

I walked as purposefully as I could up a steep hill and soon came to Queen Street, the third main street of Edinburgh's New Town. Queen Street was planned as a mirror image of the better-known Princes Street. It's bordered on its north side by gardens, and on its south side by Georgian houses whose capacious halls were designed so that a sedan chair could be brought right inside, the lady could descend, without getting her gown or slippers muddy, and her bearers could turn her chair around and leave again. On a plaque on the wall of one of these houses I saw the name 'Penumbra'.

Because I knew Penumbra is an organization which understands mental health problems, I decided I would ask if they had any information about schizophrenia. I rang the bell.

I received a warm welcome. The person I spoke to said that, no, they couldn't give any information about schizophrenia, but they encouraged me to carry on along Queen Street, out to the West End, to the office of the National Schizophrenia Association – not a long journey, but one which I needed so much help to make. We have milestones on our journeys, but we also have places of refuge and that's what Penumbra provided for me that afternoon. I was treated generously – not as an interfering relative who's somehow trying to take on the role of the professionals. The meeting was brief but I have never forgotten it.

I have mentioned already that Penumbra is a voluntary, 'not for profit' organization which recognizes that institutional care is seldom the long-term answer for anyone. It aims to provide a 'needs-led' service and offers a holistic approach, seeking the best possible services tailored to peoples' individual needs.

A meeting place for minds
much buffeted;
a place of calm. No pressure,
space to explore, to make.

Making mends frayed ends.

When communication fails
we fondle cats –
or reach for a pen.

There's humour, coffee, encounters, friends.

Busy people keep appointments,
draft agendas, plans,
make profits, ulcers – doubtful gains.

There is solace in the meeting place of minds.

That poem celebrates the ordinary meeting points of
daily living – coffee, talk or simply being together –
because this is where we walk with the risen Lord, the
one who speaks tender, homely words to a little girl
awakening from sleep.

When you are hurt, you learn to be gentle with the
sore bits of you. When we live with hurts, our horizon
shrinks, but, it may be, we see the things which really
matter. Someone who sits in a wheelchair observes in
fine detail the things the rest of us rush over. A friend
whose husband had been struck down with a heart attack
wrote, 'we focus on the things he can still do and are glad
of them'. I suppose that, too, is what Brother Roland
means by 'bumbling': being glad of little things and being
grateful.

Here's a snapshot of me sitting beside the rag-bag of
my life, hunting for warmth and comfort in humdrum
things. The opening words of the poem come from

Shakespeare's *King Lear*. Lear is having a tiff with one of his daughters. He tells her, 'You wear gorgeous clothes, but for some people it would be gorgeous just to be warm': 'If only to go warm were gorgeous', the old king says. I've punned on words for clothes and their making in this next poem.

An Old-fashioned Morality Yarn

'If only to go warm were gorgeous', thunders Lear:
and if comfort seems threadbare,
its tatters are covering and care
when there's nothing else to wear.

So torment yourself no more
with what you cannot repair.
Well-tested materials are to hand
to darn and patch and mend.

Joy and gratitude
fashion cloth of easy plenitude
to be worn in company or solitude –
a habit homely and rare.

Joy and gratitude, taking delight in a glimmer of sunlight – that's what Roland calls bumbling. I've also seen 'bumbling' described as kenosis, self-emptying. I'd like to stay with this theme a moment longer because this kind of unfussed approach is vital for those who have been devastated by darkness. Those little, ordinary moments which can be wondered at, laughed at, have become major signposts on my pilgrimage. I'd like to share another short poem on that theme before we continue on our way towards my encounter with the National Schizophrenia Fellowship – that encounter which the welcome I received at Penumbra did so much to enable.

> For paternosters – a pen,
> a patchwork of words.
>
> Gloria! Sunlight transfigures
> a wintry world.
>
> I choose amber
> to bead my bright fingers.
>
> A blackbird trills:
> > Magnificat!

The idea that the pattern of the daily round can help us find our hidden strengths is behind the work of Penumbra. 'We do not set out to change people but aim to provide as much support as possible to enable people to lead an ordinary life in the community.'

Penumbra opened its first house in Edinburgh in 1985, providing a home for seven people. It now provides supported accommodation for over 160 tenants in 67 different houses throughout Scotland. People from the Western Isles, for example, whose nearest psychiatric hospital is in Inverness, are separated from family, friends and their home community. A home in Lewis brought them back to their roots.

Recognizing the importance of music and art in restoring a lost sense of self-worth, Penumbra encourages the tenants of its houses to find personal satisfaction in self-expression. An activities worker specializes in making the tasks of everyday life special. 'It's about discovering the hidden in everyday things of ordinary living and looking at them in a new way', said this worker.

The original Gaelic-speaking people of the Highlands and Islands apparently knew this secret. Every action of daily living – kindling the fire, washing, putting on one's clothes, entering or leaving a house – was accompanied by a prayer or a blessing. These people were driven from their homes long ago in a terrible holocaust – literally, their landlords' men set fire to the turf roofs of their houses. The green glens of the north and west were filled with smoke.

> The land is empty now,
> only roofless homes remain – bleak heaps of stones.
> Rowans grow where women once smoored peats.
> No need now for the cruisie's glow,
> or hospitality.
> The hosts have gone, and gone with them,
> the songs. . . .
>
> . . . Their craft was art,
> each chore a song,
> each song the rhythm of a people's life. . . .
>
> Few folk are left, fewer have the language.
> Summer-long exhaust fumes blacken silent glens.
> Magnates pipe their profits southwards,
> sell Gaeldom, prepacked in tartan wrapping,
> Bed-and-board is pricey.
> Brigit with her Fosterling,
> Mary, Virgin of the Blessings,
> footsore Christ
> and Colum kindly
> can't afford to stay.

From Lament for the Land, *Beyond the Border*,
Chapman Publishing, Edinburgh, 1989

'The God of life and He only knows all the loathsome work of men on that day', declares Catriona Nic-a-Phil, telling of the forcible shipping away of whole populations from the Highlands and Islands 150 years ago.

Such forced emigration, which we now call 'ethnic

cleansing', comes about because people are felt to be surplus to requirements, but, in fact, no one is redundant. It's particularly important to realize this when we deal with mental illness. A moment's attention can be a real signpost for someone. At least, that's how I felt when the people at Penumbra welcomed me and helped me continue on the journey I didn't want to make. The way was less dark now and the sense of companionship was comforting.

I found the office of the National Schizophrenia Fellowship. I announced myself through the intercom system. 'You won't know me,' I explained, 'but my daughter . . .' – by now I was starting to cry.

The sense of sorrow stayed with me as I climbed up three flights of stairs to the office. There literature was available. As it happened, the office was low in stock, but I was given newsletters of the National Schizophrenia Fellowship and – here was the breakthrough – a book entitled *Coping with Schizophrenia: A Guide for Families*. It was about to go out of print. There were two copies left and I bought them both. I went home and devoured the book. For the first time I was receiving appropriate advice about how I should react or not react to some of the typical signals of schizophrenia.

I put the second copy in an envelope and posted it first class to Elaine's great friend, Carol. Carol is ten years older than Elaine. We met her when Elaine was 13. We loved her vibrancy, her honesty. Soon she became Elaine's confidante and friend. When, to her bitter disappointment, the school stopped teaching Spanish at the end of Elaine's first year, Carol, a graduate of Spanish and Italian was there to pick up the pieces. Being home-based with two small daughters, she was glad of this input into her own life and Elaine was marvellously competent in the house. In those days, whatever she put her hand to flowered. Carol remembers how Elaine would take over at fraught times when meals had to be got and young children were tired and fractious. Elaine has childminded for Carol and, when Elaine became ill, Carol never gave up on her, even when she received phone calls which were eight minutes of silence, Elaine at the other end being too full of despair to speak. That's why I sent Carol that second copy of the book. Outside the family, she was the main carer in Elaine's life. She phoned me at once. 'That book came this morning. I can't put it down. Now I understand why Elaine reacted the way she did before she was on medication, why she put the phone down on me, why she was so switched off from the kids. I understand much, much better now how to cope when we're together.'

It was as though a light had been switched on in a dark room, quite literally. I phoned my sister. She said, 'You're beginning to live, talk, breathe schizophrenia.' 'It's because I've just found out about it', I explained. 'I know,' she agreed. 'It's like my friend Anne when she discovered both her daughters are diabetic. For a while that's all she could talk about. Talking helped her come to terms with it.'

There's another step I needed to take, however. I have said that on my travels I have been given a souvenir I didn't like, the blessing of sorrow. That means that, as well as naming my hurts, I have to accept them and grow within them. That was the thought in the poem with the line 'hold the hand which moulds your pain'. It could be called embracing hurt. Another fairytale comes to mind: Beauty and the Beast. For the sake of her frightened father, who has stolen the Beast's rose, Beauty agrees to marry the Beast. Her love destroys his ugliness. He becomes a handsome prince.

I can't embrace schizophrenia, nor ever believe it will turn into a handsome prince, but in the Gospels I found a landmark on my journey and I put it into the poem which follows.

Silences Deeper Than Thought

Everyone went home, but Jesus went to the
Mount of Olives (John 8.1, *Good News Bible*)

Night time is best.
The blanket of stars, the world at rest.
You lean forward, stir dying ash,
but even that moment is caught
in silences deeper than thought

when every heart's breath
is a rung of a ladder climbing to God,
and you wait. To wait is to know
the drift of planets like flurry of snow,
whisper of multitudes, hugeness of space.

Yet knowing, you do
nothing, just wait. For waiting
is action, mends the things action broke,
as the woodworker once, masts, oars,
    splintered yoke.

Alone in the hills you make night your home:
dawn breaks on citadels where men hurl
    judgements like stones.

'Waiting is action.' I wasn't thinking specifically of Elaine
when I wrote that poem, but it applies to schizophrenia.
The original term, coined by a psychiatrist called Beuler,
means 'splitting' or 'splintering'. Action becomes impossible. Without wanting to, I nag Elaine constantly – to
clean her teeth, smoke less, sort out her bills, her messy
house, her life. . . . I have to learn patience, above all else.
Patience to try to safeguard the mind which action broke,
and not 'hurl judgements like stones'. It's not easy!
    Someone who has just come off the phone and only

knew Elaine slightly and pre-illness said, 'When you think of Elaine, you think of sunshine and laughter.' Someone else asked me, 'What remains of the pre-illness Elaine?' I replied, without hesitation, 'Her sense of humour!'

Here is Elaine now in summer 1992. She has styled her hair and put on a beautiful blouse. She has just been to town to have her portrait taken by a leading photographer, an action she has initiated. She plans to give this portrait to Carol and her family for Christmas and now she is posing for her brother's camera in the walled garden of the New Town flat we have been lent.

The appointment with the photographer isn't the only event in Elaine's life. She has been accepted on a hair-dressing course (Elaine has always enjoyed doing hair). And, most interestingly, she's been writing away to 'lonely hearts' columns in various papers. She's currently checking out a Classics graduate, a son of the manse and a super-market manager, and keeps us entertained with the letters in which they introduce themselves and enclose their photographs.

By the end of the summer, Elaine has made her choice. None of the original three. I shall call him Gary. She moves into supported accommodation, enrols in Italian classes and is looking forward to beginning the hairdressing course. She is still on 'leave of absence' from the hospital, under the Section 18, but her psychiatrist has agreed that she can go to her local GP for injections. The last thing I do before my return to St Petersburg is to make sure she has registered with a practice close to her house.

And can you guess what happens? She doesn't turn up at the new practice for her medication, even though she is under a court order. She sinks right back, stops the Italian classes and abandons the hairdressing course. The only thing which isn't abandoned is her relationship with Gary.

Carol and Elaine's brother phone the practice to voice their concerns. They are told in no uncertain terms that it's none of their business. In the end I have to phone the psychiatrist from Russia. That provokes action, but by then it's mid-November and Elaine has lost all the ground she had gained during the summer. She's taken back into hospital – the 'revolving door' syndrome is blighting us once again. She is so annoyed about this enforced return to hospital that she runs away and heads off to stay with her grandmother. The police chase Elaine across Lothian into Argyll.

All this hassle, all this expense to the community and, most tragically, all this lost ground in Elaine's own life could have been avoided if, instead of being told to report to the GP each fortnight, Elaine had been given a community psychiatric nurse who would have visited her to give the all-essential injection.

Eventually this service was provided and I can only repeat that it is a lifeline for Elaine and for ourselves.

So, Elaine moved into a more positive place again, though never to where she was the previous summer. Here is an extract from a letter written to me on the eve of her twenty-third birthday, from the supported accommodation where she was at her happiest. She was about to move into another house run by the same association.

Today is August 10th, the day before my birthday, I hope to celebrate it in style. . . .

Carol came round last night and we were exchanging problems and news when the new girl came in. She didn't even say 'Hello' and continued to be as surly as ever. Perhaps there's a reason for this but I can't see why. All I notice is the bad vibes I get from her. (I think, I'll be glad to move).

Went back to Carol's and had pasta and Malibu. Walked through Leith this afternoon and got sunburnt but felt very happy none the less. Came back to prepare dinner for the house meeting (three-course meal).

Yesterday wasn't so hot, though, I almost felt as if I was cracking up in the afternoon, so I went for a walk to make myself feel better.

Angela has moved on and it's very quiet and dull without her. It was reassuring to know her rather large bulk was always around.

My darling brother is taking me out for lunch tomorrow for my birthday and the Scobrod [her nickname for Gary, the new boyfriend] is coming at night.

By the way I had a visit from the Mental Welfare Commission, so I complained about various things to do with that intolerable hospital. It's funny how things swing full circle in life. Perhaps people are realizing the effect or damage they've had on my life. I still wish it was plain sailing, though.

Going back to the Welfare Commission, Mark (a support worker) says it's a terrible system to get embroiled in. Long live end of Section day! Freedom from the legalities?

Must fly, should have put the dinner in the oven half an hour ago.

P.S. We've just had a house meeting which went well. . . . I sometimes question my own basic living skills, it's one of things which got so undermined, hence the lying in bed all day. But then we come back to the shattered self-image where your basic self is still alive, however poor, whereas the ego can be deflated or inflated by circumstances and people. That part of us (the self) is intrinsic and a directive to the way we live. I hope you find this as interesting as I do. What I'm trying to say is that progress in a process of self-realization is being made.

Happiness is derived from self-fulfilment and satisfactory relationships. What more could I ask for in life? Having said that I stand at a disadvantage, knowing that what should be intrinsic in me is no longer there. Other props and struts that go to make up a life have been removed – things like drive and ambition have been pared away – and being good at what you do when there is nothingness.

Elaine's perception of herself in that letter is mirrored in the portrait she had taken. She faces the camera, her chin propped on her left hand. Her hair, clothes, make-up are flawless, but her eyes tell another story. I avert my gaze from eyes which have looked into the nothingness of which she writes.

I don't want to focus on that nothingness. As Elaine writes, she is in a more serene place. She has found delight in going for a walk, in cooking a meal, in satisfactory relationships. 'What more could I ask for in life?' she asks herself. I shall close this chapter with a poem which I wrote in Russia. I sent it to Elaine and she took great delight in it. Although it's about a painting in the Russian Museum in St Petersburg, it's also about my gentle daughter for whom tranquility is so often, alas, a distant dream.

Reverie

(after a painting by Pavel Tchistiakov (1832–1919),
Giovanina Seated on the Windowsill, 1864,
Russian Museum)

Her eyes tranquil with reveries, a girl
muses, becalmed. The sky's oyster shell
beyond rooftops reveals its luminous pearl.
Her window is open to the first glimmer of dawn.
She is morning's sentinel: vigilant on the sill
she watches, not distant vistas, nor shadows below,
nor mists, drifting, dissolving – her gaze is within,
guarding thoughts all her own. She does not know
her reflection shimmers, mirror-like in the pane
against which her shoulders repose. Seated so,
she is glimpsed by a painter, early astir,
who spreads out his canvas to capture her dream.

CHAPTER 7

'Like Dew, Dancing'

You felt your baby burgeon and begin
her hidden life, unfurl, a tender leaf,
an embryonic print across a screen.
Her perfection assured you that her life
was worth the swollen months, the throes which join
our human race; for those who lack and those
who have enough must rear their young, must learn
uncertain grace notes: love and hope. The rose
which blossoms from the bud shows what we are,
though prickles tear, mildew and maggots blight.
Our risks, our hurts, mistakes still chart the star
we aim for, graph our path through dark and light.

Your little daughter teaches, foetal, blind,
that frailty is strength which makes us kind.

Beyond the Border, Chapman Publishing, Edinburgh, 1989

At the beginning of June 1995, Stuart and I returned
from Russia for the summer, as usual. Friends met us at
the airport, and with them was our son. If we'd taken any
photographs, they would have shown that Stuart looked
drawn and unwell. Later we learned that he had a breakdown of his immune system, including hepatitis. But the
photographs then would have shown smiles as we were
welcomed by our friends.

'Where's Elaine?' I wondered.

My son drew me to one side. 'Elaine's in hospital. She was taken off medication because she's pregnant. Things got so awful she phoned her CPN and asked to be admitted.'

'So, she really is pregnant?'

'Yes, three months. They can start the medication again, but the bad news is that it was 4.30 on a Friday afternoon. Not a lot could be done over the weekend, and you know how she hates that place. The good news is that at least she got in touch with someone.'

'Yes,' I agreed. 'At least she looked for help.'

'She's homeless. The housing association kicked her out. She'd got so ill she was upsetting other people. Then she left a cigarette burning in her room and set the place on fire. They had to call the fire brigade. She'll have to stay in hospital until she can get somewhere to live. She's been in touch with the Housing Department.'

Our daughter was sick and homeless, expecting her first child. I phoned the hospital that evening to speak to her on the patients' phone.

The next day I went across town to see Elaine.

It was a horrible day, the sort of day that makes people say, 'It's not the British winters that make people want to emigrate, but the British summers.' The rain was coursing down the hospital windows, making that gloomy place gloomier than ever.

We sat together on Elaine's hospital bed, curtaining ourselves off from a bizarre woman who was yelling obscenities.

'So you really are pregnant?'

'It's a girl. They say it's definite that it's a girl. Look.'

She reached for her handbag and showed me a tiny etching, a little feather of life, curled up and growing. Tears came to my eyes as I looked at the computer printout of our little granddaughter. 'Oh!' I said and our eyes met and I smiled through my tears. 'Oh, she's beautiful, Elaine, oh, how wonderful.'

I think the angels in heaven wept to see my daughter radiant with her pregnancy in the drab psychiatric ward.

'They want me to take medication,' she said and started to cry. Through her tears I heard her ask a question. 'Am I . . . ?'

I thought I had heard her words, but I bent closer. 'Are you what, dear?'

She brushed me away. 'Nothing, Mum.'

'Am I . . . ?'

'Am I . . . ?' she whispers.

Summer rain streaks
the barred windowpane,
mascara runnels her cheeks.

I am close as her heart's breath
yet I cannot reach her,
adrift on the deeps.

Together we affirm,
etched on a scan,
the shape of her child, forming within –
bone of our bone, fibre and brain.

Outside, the wind weeps.

The doctors allowed Elaine to come home with me. We were living in a 'room and kitchen' flat, our toehold in the housing market. It's very centrally situated and surrounded by little corner shops which stay open forever, but it was overcrowded when Stuart and I moved back each summer.

When Elaine stayed the night, she had to sleep on the settee in the kitchen – the same settee on which she had slept away so many, many hours of her late teens.

We talked about housing – and also about wedding plans, for Elaine was sure she and Gary wanted to get married. They had got engaged the summer before.

The big question, which we could raise but not answer, was voiced by a friend who wrote rejoicing with me at the news of our coming granddaughter and hinting delicately from her experience (she's a psychotherapist) that 'It may be hard for Elaine to care for the baby.' In fact, while Elaine was still a patient in the hospital my husband and myself were called for an interview with the Consultant who warned us, 'She may not be able to look after her baby.'

I don't know if Elaine was told this. She certainly wasn't included in the discussion the doctor held with us and, even at that interview, no care plans were discussed. Social workers would be involved, we were told.

Because she was homeless, pregnant and with a mental health problem Elaine was likely to be given a flat, but, of course, it could be anywhere in the city. However, a lovely thing happened. She was allocated a flat in our own area. It was in a tower block, south-facing, with a balcony and stunning views over the city – a tremendous panorama of Arthur's Seat, the Castle, right across to the Pentland Hills.

Now we had to plan the wedding. It was at the end of July, on a beautiful summer's day, just 12 days before her twenty-fifth birthday.

Elaine wore lace, a flamenco-style dress inspired by her time in Seville. At her marriage service we rejoiced in, and prayed for, the unborn child. It was a time of joy and affirmation and when it was over I wrote her a poem.

To Elaine: Her Story, Her Birthday

The moment of your making
was firelit, curtains drawn
against dark winter:
there was gentleness and joy.

Joy through nine months
anticipation together.
We both grew full of bloom. . . .
I loved you before I saw you,
bonded with you as you came.

Tuesday's child, fair of face,
you blossomed beside our hearth, our herb of grace,
grew tall and slender,
played among the ebbings of sea and sunset
in lonely places in the west.

This summer we shared a wonder:
an etching, a shape on paper —
the curl of life within your womb;
and the sky laughed roses
as you stood gorgeous among folds of lace
in the presence of the angels
for the marriage of child, bride and groom.

If only words could mend the mind action broke! I began
a quest for help for Elaine. I couldn't anticipate what the
exact difficulties would be, but, as I sat in our flat among
packed suitcases, ready to return to Russia, I phoned a
senior psychiatric social worker. 'Had he', I queried, 'ever
known of a situation in which a mother with schizophrenia successfully cared for her child?'

'I've known only three cases,' he told me, 'and in each

there was massive back-up from Social Services and from the family.'

But Stuart and I were living abroad. My twin gave Elaine a lot of help, coming down at weekends during her pregnancy, buying necessary things for the baby, packing Elaine's bags ready for hospital. People at church passed on things, of course, and Carol and her family were fully involved. Elaine had already asked Carol and Paul to be godparents and their three daughters were looking forward to the arrival of their new 'godsister'.

So were we! A fax came to Russia. 'Elaine and Gary have had a gorgeous wee daughter, Margaret Fiona, born by Caesarian section.'

I booked a flight home, planning to arrive a day before Elaine's return from hospital with her baby.

My sister met me at the airport. Her face was shining. 'I've seen your granddaughter, Jenny. She's beautiful. Just wait till you see her.'

I was still half in Russia, trying to focus but barely taking things in as we drove along the Queensferry Road in the winter dark towards my daughter's flat.

'So Elaine's home?' I queried. 'I thought she wasn't getting out until tomorrow.'

'I know, that's what I thought, too, but she signed herself out. They let her go with her baby, even though she had "severe schizophrenia" written on her medical notes, imagine it. She phoned me yesterday afternoon, she said she was worried, Margaret was sleepy. She's jaundiced and it makes babies sluggish.'

I nodded, my eyes on the road ahead, trying to take everything in.

'I told her she was right to be concerned. I phoned back later. I could hear Margaret crying so I thought, that's all right, at least she's awake. But Elaine still couldn't get her to feed properly. It's awful, Jenny. They've got no heating, just an electric fire, and no hot water. Elaine should be having daily baths after her operation, but it's as though she's in another world. The Community Midwife's been. She's doing all she can to keep the situation under control. Things were slipping out of hand but it's OK now. Margaret's had two feeds of water. Otherwise they'd have rushed her into hospital. The midwife brought bottles of sterilized milk. She's on three-hourly feeds.'

We lugged my case into the lift. I'd bought a box of soggy cakes from Russia, wanting to bring something to celebrate the homecoming. It was a mistake. They were totally bashed to bits.

'Come and see the baby', my sister said.

We looked to the young parents for their consent.

'Of course', Elaine and Gary agreed.

My sister took my hand and led me into the main bedroom. A little Moses basket, passed on by Carol, was resting on a bundle of clothes on the floor beside the bed and inside was the scrap of babyhood which was to change all our lives.

For the first moment I held back. She was Elaine's and Gary's, after all. 'Pick her up, cuddle her. She's yours. She's your little granddaughter. Isn't she beautiful?' my sister said. I called through to Elaine. 'Can I pick her up?' I lifted Margaret from the cot – and do I need to say any more?

She was born just before the season of Advent, so there were winter poems for Margaret. I wrote in between feeds, the cuddles and loves, the talking and the bathing, the housework, the nurture of my granddaughter – and her mother, too.

Seagulls swoop outside the high-rise room,
travellers from shores where cold tides crest
    and foam.
Pedestrians bear trees and tinsel far below.

Sun and snow about bare hills and spires show
how wise to wait:
grow hiddenly towards the birth we celebrate.

How generous the ebb and flow of
    storm-washed sun
whose light outlines the city's silhouette
this time when righteousness and truth
    have met –
and the earth buds a fragile blossom,
a winter bloom.

I read that poem to Elaine. Her response was to pick up
a pen and write.

Daughter Margaret with your ways and habits,
you bring a smile of joy to your parents.
An island princess – you were named to bless you.
From the moment I knew you were inside me
I felt joy from the bottom of my soul.
The protection I gave you right from the start
is what made you so bright and alert,
and in awe I watched your tiny frame.
So what do you think of the world that you see,
of Granny and Mummy and all of us three?
Secretly you were knit and secretly you smile,
the ways of a cherub who's destined to be
high above us all eternally.

I've pasted Elaine's poem next to Margaret's first ever
photograph which Elaine had taken in hospital. Her eyes

are shut, her wee fingers are curled above the blanket and you can just make out the lettering 'Royal Infirmary' in red around her white hospital gown! You can also see a very determined look in that newborn face.

Here are the last two lines of another poem from me, a Christmas one for Margaret:

Children with eyes full of wonder came
and clustered, hushed, about the Christmas flame.

I struggled with that last line. I wanted to use the Orkney word, 'peedie', meaning 'little', in this Nativity poem for my small granddaughter. My grandmother came from the Orkney Islands, from the Isle of Stronsay. Elaine and her brother love the west coast, but my twin and I feel a great sense of homecoming in Orkney.

The Orkney word didn't fit, but poems for Margaret soon came winging their way from those windswept islands. For in Orkney lived a poet called George, whose thoughts were with our little trio, Elaine, Margaret and Gary. 'I remember them when my candle is lit,' he wrote.

Angels visited Margaret in the form of prayers and gifts and poems. Pigeons flew about the window and settled on the balcony and our little dove nestled in our arms and cooed her content.

But all was not well. Daddy Gary was proud of his daughter, but it was all too heavy for him. Elaine was far from well, mentally, and now mother-in-law had landed herself on them. It's not surprising the young father found it hard to handle.

I had come home for a month, but I realized that Elaine needed continuing support to care for Margaret, so I stayed on. Once Margaret was (mostly) sleeping through the night, I started overnighting in our own flat where my son lived, coming down each morning on the first bus in time to see the first red of frosty dawn touch the shoulder of Arthur's Seat, to hear birdsong from the scrubby rowans far below – and to see our wee fledgeling stirring in her little nest.

Sometimes I would see that a bottle had been given in the night, that the baby had been lifted and put back in the cot – Gary's doing, I was sure, even though he left early for work in the morning.

Two social workers visited – a senior psychiatric social worker from the hospital who brought a social worker from the community.

'Hello, I'm Pam. I want to tell you, Elaine, that I'm nothing to do with mental health. In fact, I don't mind telling you, you probably know more about mental health than I do. I'm here to support you and your baby. It's the policy of our department to keep mothers and babies together.'

I saw Elaine's face. On the one hand, disbelief that it could be thought that she might need any help to care for her much-loved baby, on the other, relief.

How bitter, later, would be the sense of betrayal!

I made them all cups of coffee.

'What sort of support can you offer?'

'A childminder', the Social Worker said.

Elaine looked absolutely dumbfounded. 'I don't need a childminder. I'm not a working mother.'

'Where would the childminder be?' I wondered.

'Craig's Castle', she said.

'But that's so hard to get to without a car', I objected.

'Oh, we might be able to organize a taxi to take you there.'

A taxi! If Elaine were able to get herself and Margaret fed, dressed and out every morning and into a taxi she wouldn't need a childminder.

'Elaine needs help in her own home', I ventured.

They made a note of this and, following this visit, the Social Work Department provided a home help. She arrived when Margaret was two months old.

On the Home Help's first visit, Elaine was having a bad day – and had no cigarettes. The Home Help walked into her bedroom. Elaine lifted her head, very much on the defensive. Nancy took no offence, but walked away to put the kettle on.

'She's needing a cigarette,' I explained.

'Is she now! I'm a smoker mysel'. I ken how it feels. Here you are, Elaine,' she said, as if she'd known her all her life. 'Have a couple of fags on me.'

They lit up together. The bonding was instant!

But Elaine was very fragile and we were worried how she would make out without my support. I had deliberately put off my return to Russia until Margaret was four months, well-established on her feeds, having had her first injections. But each new stage of development brings new worries. The Social Work Department agreed to increase the home help input in the month in which I would be away to include an hour at bedtime as well. But what about the hours between Nancy's departure at 11 and her return at 5.30?

'I'll take Elaine and Margaret up to me,' Carol decided. 'It's the school holidays, so all the kids will be at home, and, once they're back at school, I'll come down every afternoon to see how things are.'

Carol lives eight miles from Elaine. At that stage, she was running her own language school from her home, timetabling her classes to fit in with school hours. It was a staggeringly generous offer to make.

My sister offered to pay for extra care over and above what the Social Work Department was offering. I was sitting discussing this with Elaine when the phone went. We heard the Social Worker's voice on Elaine's answering machine. 'Hello, Elaine, Pam here. Sorry I've missed you. Please phone back as soon as you get in.'

Elaine looked at me rather strangely. 'The authorities are interested in me, Mum.'

'Oh?' I said, 'then we'd better phone back.'

'No, no, you don't need to phone back.'

But I did, and the Social Worker told me that Elaine had made a call to the Department earlier. 'She said she was worried about her baby, that the police were in her home tampering with her baby's brain.'

I wasn't surprised. Elaine was far from well. At New Year she had overdosed. I had told community psychiatric nurses, her Consultant and the social workers themselves that Elaine needed help. Indeed, after the overdose, I was led to believe that the medication would be increased, but nothing happened and she became more and more unwell. Ten days previously she was convinced her husband had put poison in her coffee. A voice from the television had confirmed this and warned her not to drink it. She put him out and phoned the police, but after a day or two she started to worry about him and they were reunited again.

'If someone thinks their baby is being tampered with', the Social Worker went on, 'the next question is, what might they do to protect their baby? We're going to admit her to hospital.'

'I'm not going,' Elaine said. 'There's no need for me to be in hospital. I phoned the Social Worker over a concern I had. I'm not ill and I can't leave Margaret.'

For the next four hours floodtides of officialdom washed through Elaine's home. The GP called with forms, but brought the wrong ones and had to call again. Social workers came, a mental health officer came, and managed to catch her fashionable boot on the flex of Elaine's phone, disconnecting us.

'If you refuse, we'll have to call the police', they warned Elaine.

Elaine looked across at me. 'Why are they calling the police?' she asked and started to cry. 'I haven't done anything wrong', she sobbed.

'I know, sweetheart, but they won't call the police if you agree to go to hospital. Tell you what, supposing Margaret and I chum you in the ambulance', I coaxed, reverting to the Edinburgh expression of her teenage years.

In the end, with terrible resignation, Elaine went into her bedroom and started putting some things into a polythene bag.

I dressed Margaret in her little red outdoor suit. Elaine carried her baby out to the lift. We went out to the ambulance which had pulled up outside. The Mental Health Officer came too. Elaine didn't deign to look at her. A gaggle of small kids clustered curiously about the doors of the ambulance, staring.

Elaine sat on one of the seats, holding Margaret against her. I longed for the doors to close and shut out the curious world.

Eventually we moved off. It felt more like a police van than an ambulance and, through the narrow windows, the city seemed an alien place, oddly disconnected.

So Elaine was admitted to hospital. I couldn't phone Gary – the phone had been damaged. I phoned the people closest to Elaine: her brother, her parents-in-law, and, of course, Carol, who showed immediate concern. 'Elaine? In hospital? I'll come and visit her tonight.'

'Oh, Carol, that's very good of you. It'll mean a lot to Elaine to see you.'

'I'll get down as soon as I can,' Carol promised. 'I must feed the family first and then I'll be right down. What about Margaret? What's going to happen to her?'

'I don't know,' I told her. 'I'm going back to Russia on

Thursday. I don't feel it's right for Elaine's and Gary's sake to take her so far away and, anyway, it's not the best place to take a small baby.'

The Mental Health Officer offered to run Margaret and me home – she needed to see Gary. But he was still out. It fell to me – and Carol who came down after her visit to Elaine – to try and reassure Gary that, although none of us wanted Elaine to be in hospital, she would at last be given the help she so clearly needed.

I spent the next day running to and fro to the Social Work Department with Margaret in the pram. We phoned the Russian Embassy, British Airways. If I wanted to take Margaret to Russia, I'd have to go to Glasgow to get her written in on my passport. It just didn't feel right to take her so far away. Oh, how I wanted to! I imagined filling my case with nappies and baby milk. I imagined carrying Margaret with me in her little chair through the airport.

Carol phoned. 'Listen,' she said, 'I'll look after Margaret. I was going to have her and Elaine for the next two weeks anyway. I've been in touch with Gary. He's agreed.'

The next day, my last day in Edinburgh for a month, I took Margaret up to the hospital to see Elaine. 'Carol's going to look after Margaret for you', I told her.

'That's all right then, but I shouldn't be in here, Mum. It should be me doing it. I'm the mother.'

She didn't want me to take her baby away. I left in tears, kissing the top of Margaret's head as I carried her home.

As I neared Elaine's high-rise flat, Carol pulled up. We packed Margaret's things, then Carol dropped me off and drove away with Margaret strapped in her baby chair.

I lay down in the little box room in our flat. I was in shock, truncated and torn apart. I spent the night in tears. Next day, on a crowded flight to St Petersburg, I broke down again. A steward passed me tissues. 'Is anything the matter, madam?'

A month later, I wept again, but these were tears of joy as Carol opened her front door to me and put my grand-daughter into my arms.

I end with a poem, wishing our wee one well.

Like Dew, Dancing

Hush! we'll mention no ill-omen
at the dawn of your being
in the garden of your babyhood
where dew dances in sunlight.

There are always thorns in the rose garden. Briar
Rose, in a palace cleared of cutting edges fell
under the curse

at bud-blossom 16.

We'll mention no hard facts.

The authorities, we are assured, ensure that
blighted ones receive 'appropriate support', but no
more resources can be poured into the topic at
this stage. . . .

So, we'll not breathe a word

lest a shadow darken your rosebud life
unfolding so gladly before us

like dew, dancing.

CHAPTER 8

'Edinburgh is shadows on one side, light on the other'

> A homeless girl,
> Christmas lights in her hair,
> cradles her child,
> armies march, torches flare.

That Nativity poem refers to Elaine, too, a young mother who loves her baby but is defenceless against the armies of paranoia, the flaring torches of oppression which invade her being.

Stuart and I are deeply wounded because schizophrenia is an illness which affects families. The following brief poem tries to sum up the devastation caused by severe mental illness in our family's life.

> First, the avalanche:
> our young girl was trapped.

> Then, the explosion:
> which left us derelict
> in rubble where windows gape
> and walls collapse.

Remember how Elaine had written in her letter to me from supported accommodation that all 'the props and struts that go to make up a life' had been taken away from her? Not surprisingly, it turned out that she was particularly vulnerable after Margaret was born. Childbirth leaves many women feeling prey to fears, victims of emotions we often cannot control. How much more when there's a history of severe mental illness? When Margaret was born, the Community Midwife, who did so much to pull a deteriorating situation together, told my sister that Elaine's Community Psychiatric Nurse had warned her colleague that Elaine could be particularly prone to relapse six or eight weeks after the birth. In spite of this, no action was taken. There was no suggestion that there would be extra psychiatric support or that medication should be increased.

My daughter's mind became a battleground for disturbingly black thoughts and fears.

The photographs in the family album show a bonny, thriving baby, a sweet young mother – and an increasingly haggard granny whose reward, however, was to see the wee one blossom. My husband was miles away in St Petersburg. Our whole future was uncertain, but it seemed more likely to be abroad than here. Yet, in those first four months of Margaret's life I was effectively her full-time carer. I pushed her pram across Leith Links, the green sward with trees and swing parks where, it's said, golf was played just as early (earlier, Leithers vow) as in St Andrews. I walked by the Water of Leith, bumping the pram over cobbles, passing the house where Mary Queen of Scots lunched on her return from France, a childless young widow of 19. I wondered desperately how I could save our situation. For Margaret to thrive, Elaine needed me beside her day and night, but I was supposed to be in Russia with my husband. I had taken time out to care for Margaret, but this couldn't be carried on indefinitely.

Nor was it fair on Gary to have Granny intruding into his home, even though I tried to make myself as scarce as possible. And so did he, by not coming home, even when I wasn't around, leaving Elaine on her own and Margaret crying. I know, because I would keep in almost hourly touch by phone from my son's flat.

Just the same, I viewed every flat in the vicinity of Elaine's tower block with new eyes. Could we live here? Could this be a home for us?

'You're trying to sustain the unsustainable', I was told. But sometimes you have no choice.

The pages of our family album have turned up a glimpse of my mother, but not yet of my father, Margaret's great-grandad. In his youth, he loved the hills – we have many sepia-coloured photographs of the peaks he climbed. But he was a heavy smoker who developed lung cancer. My twin and I were both expecting our first babies when the doctors drew us aside and gave us a very dark prognosis.

Do you believe in miracles? My father didn't know he had cancer, but he did know that at home he had a wife with a progressively disabling illness, Parkinson's disease. He lived to look after her – and he lived for ten more years. As I pushed the pram around Leith I saw in my little granddaughter's face a resemblance to the great-grandparent she would never know. The likeness produced a poem.

'Your father is heroic,' doctors said.
'Who once climbed Highland bens,
now gasps his way along scrubbed corridors
to tend the wife he 19 years has nursed.'

We are a family, it seems, for marathons.

Twenty years later I scale
an insurmountable precipice,
toil
over the broken scree
of my daughter's injured mind.
And, in a heart-stopping rush
in the infant eyes
which gaze up from the pram I push,
I recognize my father's steady look.

My granddaughter is thus so poignantly known!
I trace her heritage in feature, smile, shape of
    every bone
and pray she will always be encircled by her own.

'She's just so perfect, such a tiny little bundle,' Elaine
wrote at that time. 'I can't get over it. I'm breastfeeding
her now and it's a nice time. She's just such a good baby.'

When I read those words, my sense of a war scenario
deepened, which is why this chapter opened with a
Nativity poem with a war setting. Jesus was born in an
occupied country whose conquering forces had enforced
a major census, displacing entire populations. His life was
at risk from earliest infancy and he and his parents had
to flee the mass killing of small children. The Wise Men
weren't really so wise when they strayed into the palace
of the king, seeking the child who lay on straw.

Muffled against winds which blew grit into their faces,
the Magi travelled in the tracks of old trade paths which
had criss-crossed the desert from time immemorial. By

day, they rested beside their kneeling camels and then, perhaps, they talked of their libraries, their learning, their charts and the courses of stars.

They had a star to guide them, but they blundered into the courts of an earthly king and blurted out the very news which brought the newborn baby the greatest danger. 'Where is the Child born to be King?'

If ever a question put the cat among the pigeons, that one did!

'Herod was very upset and so was everyone else in Jerusalem', writes Matthew in what must be one of the biggest understatements in Scripture.

We all make mistakes which cause us great anxiety – and may even do serious harm. When we're totally devastated, the last story we ever think of turning to is the one of the Wise Men with their star-led questing, their exotic gifts, but this story reassures us that things work out in spite of our mistakes. Jesus is saved from Herod's clutches, although (and it's a very big 'although') Herod ruthlessly murders other baby boys, an act of calculated violence which looks back to Pharoah and forward to two millenia of pogroms and destruction.

In his death on the cross, Jesus will atone for the murderers who tore babies from the mothers of Jerusalem and massacred them. In his death too are encompassed millions – too many millions – of other slaughters: Auschwitz, Babi Yar, the killing fields of Cambodia, Bosnia, Rwanda, a gym hall in Dunblane, little James Bulger, Jade Matthews . . . There are too many deaths, too many tears, too much blood. They are as much part of the Jesus story as gold, frankincense and myrrh. The crying of the innocent is still the voice of God.

Walking a knife edge in those first months of Margaret's little life, I was amused to learn that a friend who lives in a nice villa, just like our former rectory, was at a weekend conference in Cambridge, studying urban theology. No snapshot here, but a poem.

Urban Theology

– should be to house theologians
in high-rise blocks
(a ladder of ascent, heaven bent)
to air their smalls
across the clouds,
converse with angels –
God's elect;
while the disadvantaged dwell
nearer to hell
in stone-built villas,
conference in plush hotels
with five-star dinners,
train politicians to repent
and take their place in Parliament.

In a more serious vein, I wrote to a friend:

Our tragedy is that Elaine loves her baby. She engages charmingly when she is feeling able to and when Margaret is smiling and happy. She speaks to her lovingly, feeds her endlessly on her breast, but a lot of the time she is unable to react at all and she cannot respond appropriately when Margaret makes demands – crying because she is unwell, teething and so on. And, of course, as Margaret starts to move about more there will be other problems.

What is needed is for Elaine to be royalty with a housemaid and nanny, who present her lovely little baby fed and cared for, for Mummy to play with, love, cuddle and talk to. At the moment it works like this:

she has a home help – and I'm the nanny.

I know the aim is to give her more responsibility – sound practice if you are dealing with a normal young mother who just needs a bit more help than usual, but tragically unrealistic in this situation. Had I not been there, our granddaughter would certainly have been removed to foster care by now.

And, in fact, that's what happened when Elaine went to hospital and I returned to Russia: Margaret's removal to Carol's home was sanctioned by the Social Work Department.

In the month in which I was with Stuart in St Petersburg – and you can guess how much anguish and heart-searching went into thinking through our whole future during that month – we heard that, although Elaine was plainly still very disturbed, an in-patient in the psychiatric ward, a decision had been made by a case conference for her to be moved to a mother and baby unit with Margaret in beside her and nurses to supervise, but not intervene in any way. Elaine, pre-illness, had been a wonderfully competent childminder, but the whole venture was doomed to failure. Can you imagine anything more inappropriate: putting a nurse in to do nothing but watch someone whose paranoia makes her feel that she's being spied on already? Yet that's what happened and Elaine still believes, nearly two years later, that the 'psychiatric people' are controlling her. 'They're in my clock,' she tells Carol and me. 'They're watching me.' And although she lives on the fifth floor, she keeps her curtains drawn to protect her against spying eyes.

Even without that element of paranoia, Elaine was far too unwell to look after a baby and Margaret, who had only been with Carol and Paul for ten days, was still very unsettled. In the end, Elaine herself asked to be moved back to the normal ward and Margaret was returned to Carol and Paul's foster care, leaving us all to feel that the whole venture had been mismanaged as well as having been mistimed.

There are enormous pressures on small children whose parents have mental illness. Parents can have unreal expectations, treating an infant like a much older child, for example. A friend in Finland told us of her neighbour's daughter. This young mother came home from hospital with a new baby and strapped her in a high chair as though she were a toddler. Or, wrapped up in overpowering thoughts, mothers may involve themselves too little in the child's life, which leads to neglect that isn't wilful, but is still neglect. A mother may misinterpret the child's crying, pick up the toddler after its sleep, for instance, and decide it needs to go back in its cot again, put it back, unchanged, still crying, walk out and shut the door, but then, absorbed in herself, she might not realize how long she has left the child alone. Or else the wee thing might show its mother some new toy, its face all smiles, and the mother may be too involved with herself to respond. If that happens once, OK, but if it happens over and over again, the child is deprived of the attention that is a basic essential in its development.

A further risk is that a child can become locked into the parent's paranoia or become the focus for their delusions. The textbook situation is when a parent projects their sense of being persecuted out to the child who either becomes an embodiment of evil or has to be protected at all costs from imagined impending doom.

There are dozens of scenarios. I've only been able to generalize here, but what we've seen has allowed us to imagine the complications involved. It's been found that the younger the child is when the parent becomes ill, the more disturbed he or she is likely to become, particularly if the illness is severe. Parents who have mental problems may not perceive that there is a difficulty or else may, understandably, be afraid to contact social workers for fear that the child will be removed from their care.

And if parents have difficulties, so do social workers. They often wait until a crisis occurs and then react with anxiety and set mothers overly ambitious targets, which they can't and don't meet, so they lose their child. We've seen that happen too.

I read papers now with eyes attuned to the needs of the mentally ill. I've read that there are counselling and befriending services for children, but it is generally agreed that what is needed is a total package of support services – help with childcare, help in the home and befriending and counselling *each* member of the family.

Is this possible? The structures are barely in place to allow someone with mental illness to live 'in the community', far less to support a family. Carol told me how the Social Worker panicked once when a minor crisis occurred with Elaine. She was shaking, she turned to Carol for support, asked for a cup of coffee, could she have a cigarette? And then she made decisions which Elaine could only have interpreted as punitive. Carol and Paul told me later that the response of the Social Work Department was too confrontational on the one hand and not far-reaching enough on the other. Perhaps it's unrealistic to think that total care would ever be possible, but it's surely better to think through an appropriate 'package of care' than to hold case conferences and, essentially, leave things as they are.

One problem was that once Margaret came into care, the Social Worker was actually there for her rather than for Elaine. Margaret's 'case' was later transferred to a more experienced social worker and the whole thing was more consistently handled, but Elaine was left without support

129

except for her Community Psychiatric Nurse. When we protested, which we did, often, we were told that Elaine refused help: she wouldn't keep appointments, she didn't answer the door or phone.

My argument is that, instead of withdrawing help from Elaine for not opening her door, the people who are providing 'care in the community' should develop the skills to circumvent their clients' refusal. Moreover, community psychiatric nurses, her indispensable lifeline, are only on call between 9 and 4.30 five days a week. If black thoughts assail her outside those hours or at weekends, she has no one to turn to, except the hospital ward where she will speak to a stranger.

There is now a day hospital in her area and she is encouraged by her Community Psychiatric Nurse to attend. There are also, I believe, 'resource centres'. But Elaine says she doesn't want to be involved with anything labelled 'psychiatric services', so she sits at home, alone.

How we appreciate gestures of friendship made towards Elaine! Friends of the mentally ill have to be sensitive in the extreme – no easy task. Conversation can be limited, even non-existent. Carol wrote to me in Russia, 'I took Elaine out for lunch. She had wanted to go out in the evening, but I felt she wasn't ready for that yet, so we went for lunch. I was quite disappointed because she was very withdrawn and other friends had said she'd seemed quite chatty and much better last week. She wanted to come home with me, but I persuaded her to go back to the hospital, but later she phoned me and told me how much she'd enjoyed her time with me even though she'd been so withdrawn.'

We've found that, too. During that winter of 1991, when Elaine was totally in another world, we went to Aberdeen to my sister's and walked by the sea in utter silence. It was the very end of December and freezing. A red sun lay low over the North Sea. We felt Elaine wasn't with us at all and, yet, all these years later, she recalls that walk, the beauty of the day and what it meant to her.

Friendship isn't very rewarding when someone is so preoccupied they seem rude, uncaring and simply downright selfish. It's not easy when trivial remarks are interpreted as major slights.

'Elaine and I went swimming with Susan,' Carol wrote on another occasion, referring to her youngest daughter. 'It was a good thing to do as Elaine didn't have to talk. She swam lengths and I played with Susan. She did get a bit impatient because I took longer getting ready than she did. She just walked off and went back to the car.'

The pre-illness Elaine would have said to Carol, 'Go on, Carol, you go for a swim, I'll stay in the baby pool with Susan.' And then she would have stayed and helped her friend dry and dress Susan.

When I write that Carol has 'held on' to Elaine through her illness, I'm well aware that this friendship is a very great gift indeed. Had she not taken our little granddaughter into her own home? Now, realizing that long-term care was being discussed with the social workers, Carol and Paul were seriously considering providing that, whether by being her guardians or by adopting her.

I returned from Russia, leaving Stuart again, in April 1995, six years after that moment when I had stood beneath the bare trees of the graveyard in the city which was still called Leningrad where I received the blessing of sorrow from a Russian monk.

I had left Scotland in tears of sadness, but now I wept tears of joy as my five-month-old granddaughter looked towards me with a smile of recognition in her face as Carol put her in my arms. 'She knows me, she recognizes me', I laughed and cried together, and Carol and Paul, rushing to get to work, to get the children to school, paused and shared my joy.

Elaine was still in hospital. I childminded for Carol, who was teaching in her own home four days a week. With her full permission, I took Margaret to see her Mummy in the mental hospital. Often I walked. Margaret and her Nan have covered many miles of her native city, all unknown to her. The Water of Leith flows near the house where she lives with her godfamily. I pushed the pram beside it and learnt that Scott's Porridge Oats had once been milled there!

We walked through Craiglockart and Morningside. We passed Napier University with its handsome, austere old building which had been a convalescent hospital in World War I for those who had been shellshocked at the Front – you can just imagine nurses with long aprons and poor broken young men taking the air in wheelchairs.

Wilfred Owen and Siegfried Sassoon met here. Owen returned to the Front and his death on the eve of Armistice, but not before he'd written what must be among the greatest war poems of all time, *Anthem for Doomed Youth*.

Schizophrenia is a war zone, too, and its victims are among the brightest and best, the most talented and sensitive of our young people, worldwide. Because they are prevented from developing, we shall never know the full extent of our loss. Parents, relatives, learn to live with worry and hurt. Friendships shrivel as sufferers become mistrustful, suspicious.

The other day, Elaine and I were driving through town, trying to help Elaine return to a flat from which she had put herself out, fearing violence, which we weren't sure had really happened. You learn to live with that, too. We passed a supermarket and started recalling times when we'd shopped there. 'Yes,' Elaine said. 'I met Ian there once, a boy from the Youth Club.' Her brother had been with her too, she said. 'He spoke to Ian, but I knew I wasn't really a somebody. My conversation doesn't carry any weight.'

'Was that when you felt that you were losing yourself?' I asked. 'That must have been so scary.'

'It was,' Elaine admitted. 'That's why I shouted at you all the time.'

'And that was distressing for us,' I recalled, 'because we didn't understand what you were going through.'

Now, though, my album is open at the page for April and May 1995, and here I am, pushing the pram with Elaine's little daughter in it through the gateway of the psychiatric hospital.

How many lost souls have drifted in here? How many mothers have, like myself, walked those long corridors in tears?

But not too many babies! Margaret brought joy to patients who were not too sunken to notice her as Elaine carried her daughter along to the canteen with me for coffee or pushed her buggy out in the gardens burgeoning with spring.

I had missed April so much in Russia. I savoured the spring flowers in gardens I passed, birdsong and the fresh green of the trees. Elaine took a photograph of me holding her baby under a tree in the grounds of the psychiatric hospital. Margaret is like a little tulip in a pink pram suit. I'm happy, holding the wee one, looking up at the sun. There's a network of branches and shadows about us.

Our small blossom saw it all, unknowing, and yet, for Elaine, it was often wintry. The long protracted business of children's panels was soon to begin, her attempts to be reunited with her baby daughter. I wrote to Stuart:

I spent two and a half hours with Margaret and Elaine in hospital. We took Margaret out in the gardens in her buggy. Elaine has to keep stopping for a smoke. We heard police cars in the distance. She said, 'Those police sirens, Mum, they're in my head, they're after me.' She disputes the Section 18 and had a court hearing in which Carol supported her. Elaine wanted to appeal against her Section, but the solicitor (who, of course, was being paid from Legal Aid whether he presented the case or not) hadn't got the documents together and put off the hearing. The whole thing was deferred for lack of evidence, so Elaine believes she's 'not mentally ill'; it's so cruel.

Elaine was formally discharged from hospital in early June and I took Margaret down to see her parents. It meant a journey on two buses, changing in town, and the same in reverse. When we got on, around 10 a.m., the bus would fill with pensioners, off into town with their bus passes. I wrote to Stuart, 'We travel wreathed in smiles. Margaret thinks everyone gets on the bus with the one aim of smiling at her, and of course the more people do, the more she smiles back.'

But there was sorrow in the smiles. I wrote, 'She's six months and one day. Six months and a day ago we waited anxiously to hear the news, to share the joy: the delivery by our daughter of a daughter. But today I take her baby in my arms knowing that proceedings are starting for my granddaughter to go into the care of the Social Work Department. Our little tot, lying so still in my arms on the morning bus is now – officially – motherless.'

Well, yes, in a way, because the fostering arrangements were being extended. The Social Work Department was looking towards a long-term solution for Margaret, and that was hard to have to take on board. But the whole thing was undergirded by the loving family mothering Margaret and keeping her in contact with her 'blood parents' and kindred. I took my granddaughter across the city several times a week to see her parents, because I didn't want her to become estranged from Elaine.

It's not easy travelling with a buggy to be collapsed, the right fare to be ready, the baby in your arms, bags spilling around, but there's a lot of goodwill around. Pensioners told me stories of their grandchildren, old ladies talked about children who were grown and far away. Young people with learning difficulties, travelling home from special centres, talked to Margaret. Young guys in jeans muscled in to help with the buggy.

Often I walked to let Margaret sleep. The spires of the Old Town, the crown of St Giles, the great Castle on its crag were spread across the city skyline, her birthright, her heritage. Away in Orkney, with poetic insight, a new poem was made for Margaret which sets my grand-daughter in her native city. It comes from the pen of George Mackay Brown, and it ends:

> Says Jenny to Margaret,
> 'Edinburgh is shadows one side, light on the other.'
> And Margaret danced in the dappling sun.

Lit by my little granddaughter's laughter, by the smiles of her parents as I brought their daughter into their too-quiet home, by the undergirding knowledge that the family she was being fostered by were about to become her godfamily, consoled by letters and poems like the one I have just quoted, I tried to hold on to sunlight and joy as I awaited the return of Stuart from Russia for the summer.

It wasn't easy. I had to withdraw from the mother role in Margaret's life. I rejoiced daily in the generosity of Carol and Paul who allowed me to continue to be her granny, but I sorrowed too for her young parents who were grieved and angry, wanting their baby back. It wasn't easy for Carol either, or for her children, who had to accept me into their home. Carol and I had been friends, but as her friendship with Elaine developed, I obviously stepped back from that and I was a virtual stranger to Carol's two younger children. Not only that, but Stuart was far away and we had no clear idea about our future.

One particularly grey, sunless day I returned home feeling dispirited and sad. I collapsed on the settee and looked at the clutter on the mantelpiece. Among my son's zany objects – a crab that cries, a trap to catch a man-eating spider – stood my wooden carving of a way-side Christ. It came from Poland and it has moved house with us many times. (George Mackay Brown wrote once, 'Your addresses change like clouds.') I said to that poor Polish Christ, 'You look even more abject than me, Lord'. I felt faith flower. It happened unasked and was almost a warm, physical sensation, and I knew that, against all the odds, there is light in the shadows and that it is within the 'dappling sun' that I dance.

CHAPTER 9

'The core defies discovery – as does the cure'

Margaret was baptized in June. Our photographs show Elaine in canvas lace-up boots and a mini skirt, watching with true maternal pride as Stuart, returned from Russia just the day before, drips water on to his granddaughter's head. Carol and Paul, Godmother and Godfather, stand beside her, and her other Godfather, Chris, is present, too. So are her Godsisters. One of them, ten-year-old Rachel, took the baptismal candle from the font and presented it to Elaine.

Afterwards, we had a meal with strawberries and cream. One photograph shows Elaine cutting the christening cake which Carol's eldest daughter, Helen, made and iced. Another shows Elaine laughing as she holds Margaret. Carol, laughing too, feeds Elaine with strawberries and cream while the baby in Elaine's arms looks up at her Mother and Godmother. That picture sums up the sustaining role that Carol plays in Elaine's and Margaret's lives.

Elaine was living for the day when her baby would be returned to her, but we knew that a stressful process of children's panels was about to begin. The promises Paul and Carol made had particular significance. Their commitment to Margaret extends far beyond what is usually required of godparents. In taking on the physical care and nurture of their Goddaughter, Carol and Paul were keying-in to what, I'm sure, the original institution 'godparent' or 'godsibling' was set up for. In the days when it was common for women not to survive childbirth, far from being a sort of honorary aunt or uncle as they are today, godparents must often have been vital carers in their godchildren's lives.

After the christening, Carol and Paul took Margaret and their children away to the west coast. Elaine joined them there, spending a holiday with the daughter she loves in the place she loves. Then Stuart and I took Elaine and Margaret to the Isle of Barra, so Margaret, at eight months, had her first experience of crossing the Minch – and thoroughly enjoyed it! Later in the summer, I had the pleasure of welcoming a friend from Russia to Scotland. We were to work together on a book, thereby extending my stay in Edinburgh, while Stuart went back to St Petersburg.

I planned to join him in October, a month before Margaret's first birthday, but, all unknown to us, a new chapter was beginning.

At the beginning of August, I went out to Roslin, to visit our friends in the Community of the Transfiguration, Roland and John. I talked about schizophrenia, knowing that Roland himself has had first-hand experience of this illness, which affected his brother. I told them of my quest to find the goodness of God in the devastation which has robbed my daughter of her youth, her beauty, her potential – and shortly will take from her the thing she values more highly than anything else: her motherhood. Roland replied very simply, 'The goodness of God is terrifying.'

This remark of Roland's reminded me of a story I had

copied into a notebook I entitled, 'The Goodness of God'. In the fraught years of conflict between the Stuart kings and the Kirk in the seventeenth century, the Covenanters, who supported the Presbyterian form of worship, were hounded into the hills, outlawed and persecuted. In the story I read, the dragoons, the soldiers of the King, murdered an outlawed preacher, a young man who had beautiful hands. Not content with murder, the soldiers took a further revenge on the preacher's elderly father. They cut off their victim's hands and showed them to the old man, asking if he recognized them. The old man replied, 'These are my son's, my own dear son's: *good is the Lord who can do no harm to me and mine.*'

I wondered if I would ever be able to say those last words and mean them with all my heart. I said to Roland, 'I don't see any signposts on the way.'

'That's part of the pilgrimage, too,' 80-year-old Roland replied.

From the brothers in their huts I went for a routine breast scan. I'd never had one before and it wasn't exactly a pleasant experience. 'No more for another three years!' I thought and forgot all about it.

Then, two weeks later, a letter arrived. It was a Saturday morning. My sister had come down for the weekend, so I wasn't alone when I received the news. I went into our other room. 'Margie, they want me to go back.' My sister was in the high bed over a cupboard. She hung over the side of the bed and I read her response in her face.

'Of course, it probably isn't anything. It says here not to worry. It happens to lots of women, but only 1 in 16 have anything.' So, we comforted one another. But suppose I was the 1 in 16?

Next morning, I saw our former neighbour, Gwynneth, at church. She works in the screening clinic. I read in her eyes things she wasn't prepared to say at this stage, but Margie and she are going to be constant supports to me! And, in fact, we were all invited for lunch, Margie and I, my Russian friend, Elaine and, of course, baby Margaret. These good friends, Chris and Gwynneth, are also part of the network of support surrounding Margaret. Chris, you will recall, is her other Godfather.

It was a rare summer's day in Edinburgh, one that was warm enough for us to sit out in the garden and eat our meal. Elaine excused herself and went into the house where she curled up on the settee and fell asleep. Her daughter, meantime, charmed everyone – and ate a full-size dinner. By mid-afternoon, of course, she needed to sleep and my twin pushed the pram a two-mile walk home to try to get her great niece to sleep.

My twin climbs Munros and runs half marathons. She has three grandsons in South Africa and she doesn't let distance keep her from them. We have a video of her looking after three lively little boys – it's exhausting just to watch. I wrote the next poem in honour of granny power, and particularly of my sister.

Grannies

Grannies are TALL, small,
round as a ball,
thin as a pin.

Grannies wear skirts which flow
or bright sports clothes,
a long scarf or shawl –
or no hat at all.

Grannies' hair may be black or brown,
purplish blue,

grey at the edges
or white all through,
snug as a cap,
or high as a crown.

Grannies may drive a car
or ride on a bus.
They live very far
or right beside us.

They may be Grandma or Granny,
Nanny or Nan,
Grandmother, Gran . . .

But whatever her name,
whether she walks or travels by train
or flies in a plane,
you may be sure, whichever Gran fits,
she loves you to bits!

Granny power has traditionally pulled babies through sickness and offered older children comfort, a listening ear, nourishing broth and a store of family sagas. Granny power is good for the granny, too! When I went back to the clinic for more scans, I reminded myself of a pledge I'd made as I'd pushed Margaret's pram among the first frost-bound crocuses last winter. I had to stay alive for at least 18 more years – preferably 20 – to see my grand-daughter grow to maturity.

At the clinic, Gwynneth talked me through the proce-dures, chatted with me in a pleasantly furnished lounge. There was a suspicious shadow on one of the scans, but I wasn't to worry, lumps and bumps don't necessarily mean cancer.

I didn't have time to worry for there was a clinic in hospital the very next day and Gwynneth was there, on

duty, but ready to take time off to talk to me in the waiting room. This time, more consultations, more decisions,
a test with a local anaesthetic and three needles. I felt the
second needle go in and tears came into my eyes. Isn't it
too much, I thought? She has schizophrenia and I have
breast cancer. The doctor had tears in his eyes himself as
he looked steadily at me and told me that the cells and
the lump were malignant. I was touched: he must give
this news to hundreds of women and still he weeps.

My first operation was a very simple lumpectomy. It
was to be done the very next day. On Gwynneth's advice,
I phoned Stuart the evening before. 'It's better that he
knows step by step,' she counselled. 'If the lumpectomy
shows that you need further surgery, he'd be all the more
alarmed.'

And, indeed, unknown to me, Gwynneth's husband,
Chris, was on the phone to Stuart, too, urging him to
come home. He came ten days later. A friend met him
at the airport and took him straight to the hospital's
oncology out-patient department by car. He was just in
time to join me to hear the diagnosis – the cancer had
spread. I would need further surgery and a package of
chemotherapy and radiotherapy.

But there's lots of hope with this sort of treatment. The
therapy is fairly prolonged and increasingly debilitating,
but the end results are generally good. So, hoping for the
very best, Stuart and I went home to our room and
kitchen flat. We had a meal and can you guess where we
headed for next? The psychiatric hospital. The difference
between the breast unit and the psychiatric hospital was,
I have to say, like going from the light to the dark.

The breast unit has waiting rooms which try not to
be functional, brightly furnished with patchwork cushions
and covers knitted or crocheted by grateful patients. In
the mental hospital there are few – if any – grateful

patients! I took some flowers in for Elaine once. They stood on her locker for weeks, dead and horrible. In the end I threw them away.

But it's far more than the surroundings, important though these are. Not so long ago, cancer was the great taboo and never talked about. Now there is total openness, the space to ask as many questions as you need to. Husbands and close family are positively encouraged to be part of the decision-making process. There are leaflets at every turn which explain the various treatments, the likely side-effects. Women who have been through treatment come into the waiting room and get to know each new patient. They make themselves available every day for further talk if it's required. And, perhaps most important of all, thrown in with your package of care is a nurse counsellor. This amazingly sensitive, experienced person gave me a number where she could be contacted at any time of the day or night, told me that no query or anxiety would be too silly or too far-fetched for her and, in the gentlest, yet most searching way possible, exposed my fears and helped me deal with them.

In the mental hospital we had been interviewed clinically by a cold man who shed no tears as he gave us the starkest possible prognosis for our daughter, gave us no space to stammer out our questions and left us to thank him and try, numbly, to come to terms with what he had said.

However, the reason for our visit to the psychiatric hospital this time was that, for the first time ever, we had been invited to a series of meetings about schizophrenia. The invitation to attend these sessions had come a few weeks earlier, at a time when I had been feeling very low. I felt I had been walking across minefields for too long and I could see no smooth ground ahead. Then, plop, through the letterbox, totally unexpectedly, news about an information group to 'look at the issues around the meaning of the diagnosis, the treatments available, community resources, and so on'.

We were both very touched when Carol said she'd like to attend the sessions, too. It underlined for us her commitment to Elaine as friend and as mother of her child.

Here's what Elaine had to say about the sessions. 'Mum and Dad are about to go to an education programme to educate them in the ways of how to support people better. I don't feel it's necessary. There's nothing they'll find out about me which they don't already know.'

I tried to get her back on track, 'The group's going to be about schizophrenia, how do you react to that, Elaine?'

'It's about schizophrenia,' Elaine repeated. 'But I don't believe that I'm suffering from it. I don't believe I'm suffering from anything but having difficulties in everyday life. Some people's lives seem to get easier and easier and better and better. You look at them and you think how do they do it, and you look at yourself and you think, well, my life's difficult and it's not what it should be so how come there's a difference? That's what we need to find out: why one person is allowed to suffer so much, why one person isn't. And I believe that only God will be able to give us the answers when we get to his Judgement Seat. He'll tell us what we've done wrong and why things happen and why he plans them to happen. But this is what's so puzzling for me because I can't possibly think why God would allow this separation from Margaret and all the cruel treatment of the hospital. But I'm very hungry now. I could do with some lunch!'

The sessions were led by a doctor and a sociology research worker, both very professional, warm and approachable. There were four families represented in the room that evening. I can truly say that the pain in the room was tangible. One of the mothers summed it all up

144

for us. 'Schizophrenia,' she said, 'means that you see a bright young person with everything to live for turn into a travesty of a human being with a can of lager in one hand and a roll-up in the other.'

From these meetings we not only learnt more facts about medication and the Mental Health Acts, we also learnt how the hospital operates its system of care. I'd visited Elaine almost every day from April till June. I'd heard the term 'close obs.' and was left to work out that it meant that Elaine wasn't allowed out on her own, even with Carol or with me, but was 'tailed' by a nurse as we pushed Margaret's buggy in the grounds. There seemed very little rhyme or reason for this close control. One day, for example, Elaine had gone on her own to a stressful meeting with social workers about her daughter's future. The day after when Carol visited with Margaret, they quibbled over allowing her to take Elaine out to buy clothes in a charity shop. 'She's on close obs.', was the explanation that was given.

It was demeaning for us all, to say the least. Now, at these meetings I learnt that, while they are in hospital, each patient is allocated a 'key worker'. How helpful it would have been to have known that before! I have to say that on one occasion when I did talk to a 'key worker', I found him singularly uninformed about Elaine's life.

These evenings at the group coincided with my moving forward for chemotherapy and caused me to reflect on the enormous contrast between the two medical units I was involved with. For one thing, I could choose not to have treatment and although, of course, doctors would do their best to persuade me to consent, I could not be compelled to. Whereas Elaine, under the Section, has no choice. That fact produced the following sonnet.

Options

I could refuse recovery, the scar
instead of breast, the mutilating knife,
and let this cancer eat away my life
and break no law. They would persuade – no more.

From her we force consent. Officialdom
invades her home – may even axe her door –
and drag her down the windswept corridor,
detain, confine. I may choose radium,

the hope of healing. We force her to agree
to jags in flesh and muscle which dispel
delusion, incapacitate and dull
as much as the disease – this mystery

which kills not life but function. The core
defies discovery – as does the cure.

The last lines of that poem highlight the fact which the
doctor in charge of our small study group pointed out: as
far as understanding schizophrenic illness goes, psychiatry
is today where general medicine was 150 years ago. Psychiatry can list and discuss some of the many symptoms and
behaviours associated with schizophrenia, but the precise
reason for them occurring is still to be discovered.

Of the four family groups represented, one mother was
there whose daughter, the youngest of 4, had 'broken
down' 17 years ago. The only information this mother
had been given, until our group meetings, was 'your
daughter has a deteriorating illness, don't push her too
much'. This woman, to all outward appearances a highly
successful 'career woman', had unshed tears in her eyes as
she told us that her daughter's condition had 'destroyed
part of her life'.

Another couple were in their sixties. They coped at home with their sick daughter once her marriage broke up and brought up both her children. We marvelled at the stamina of this granny, whose grandchildren called her 'mum' and called their own mother by her Christian name, if they spoke to her at all. The 15-year-old daughter of this family, we learnt, was ashamed of the withdrawn shadow of a person who inhabited their front room. She wouldn't bring schoolfriends home. We could understand that reaction and could only hope that wouldn't happen with Margaret. Carol has been generous enough to continue to call Elaine 'Mummy'. We hoped that the fact that Margaret is growing up secure and confident in another family, far from alienating her from her mother, will do the opposite and awaken in the growing girl compassion for and acceptance of a mother who loves her so dearly.

The third group was a close and supportive family whose son, in his late teens, had just been diagnosed.

Whatever the duration of this illness we had experienced, we were all trying to come to terms with it. Can you ever 'come to terms' with such a thing? We were all in pain — we didn't have to say so, we expressed it in our body language, in the tears we didn't shed because we have shed too many but which were there in our throats, behind our eyes.

I have scribbled in my notes that 60 per cent of sufferers either live with relatives or receive a high level of care from their relatives. It's been found that a third of all relatives of sufferers of schizophrenia develop increased levels of anxiety, that there are not only financial implications of shouldering the 'burden of care', but also social ones. The stigma of mental illness means that sufferers and their families are frequently discriminated against. We had all been made to feel that we were 'meddlers' when we tried to get help for our loved ones.

With statistics like this, it's not surprising that we were unanimous in agreeing that the community psychiatric nurse service is absolutely vital. 'CPNs are marvellous,' we all agreed.

Those sessions gave us support and information. We could have continued as an informal group, but two of the family groups, stimulated by the course, went on to attend meetings held by the National Schizophrenia Association and found their own support there.

As far as Stuart and I were concerned, our future was too uncertain for us to take on any other commitments. We basically had only one green light: go forward for treatment. I had my therapies ahead of me, Stuart had a new course of studies opening up, we needed to find a better base for a longer-term stay in Edinburgh and Carol had the continuing care of our granddaughter to add to her own three daughters' needs.

During the sessions we were all excited by news of research in Inverness. My sister phoned to tell me about it. 'Jenny, listen, they think schizophrenia is linked with an imbalance of fatty acids in the brain – remember we read something about it in that newsletter from the NSF? Well, it's in *Scotland on Sunday*,' my sister went on. 'They hope to develop a new drug which deals successfully with the negative symptoms. It's being researched by a doctor called Iain Glen. They hope it'll be on the market within four or five years.'

By now we were both in tears. I rushed out and bought *Scotland on Sunday* and read the article, weeping.

The result was I wrote to John Major, begging for funding for this new research.

Dear Mr Major,

You are so right to speak out against waste and inefficiency! Those two words provoked me to write to you after a private hell which is set to last for as long as my afflicted daughter lives – unless the important discoveries of Dr Iain Glen and others involved in phospholipid research can be expedited. Which requires funding.

The illness which robs my daughter not of life, but of function has had more publicity in your term of office than at any other time. It is schizophrenia and in her article in *Scotland on Sunday* about Dr Glen's work, Catherine Devaney quotes Dr Silvano Areti:

'No war in history has produced so many victims . . . no other condition that we know of has deprived so many young people of the promise of life.'

Yet until Dr Glenn's findings were published, the cause of this illness remained as unknown as when Shakespeare immortalized Ophelia.

Research has highlighted the devastation this illness brings families. My husband is a priest. We carried the wounded ones of society on our shoulders. My daughter's descent into despair closed our doors. The build-up was slow and insidious. . . . Now, at 25, her appearance is slovenly, the baby she loves is in foster care and her life is almost without event, except to reach for the next cigarette, attend the next children's panel, the next Sheriff Court and hear yet again that she must take the medication which makes her sluggish and depressed. Failing to understand her illness, plagued by voices – even on medication – she can only see herself as victim of some awful plot from which there is no escape.

149

What is the cost to the State of keeping her at this minimal level of function? She receives Disability Living Allowance, she has a community psychiatric nurse, a mental health officer, a consultant psychiatrist, frequent prolonged spells in hospital, often with police officers bringing her into hospital. She has at least two social workers. And they all agree that the input they can meaningfully give is absolutely minimal because the illness which robs her of insight as well as responsibility is incurable. Her story can be multiplied six million times all over Britain – and so can the cost to the community. My plea to you is to expedite a speedier breakthrough in this devastating illness which is an enormous cost to the community as a whole but especially to young people who, through no fault of their own, are immured in a nightmarish world of suspicion and silence. And to bring mental health care and concepts from Dickensian dark ages into the twenty-first century before that century fully dawns.

My impassioned letter produced a brief reply two months later. I was assured that the authorities do all they can to ensure 'appropriate support', but no more resources can be poured into the topic at this stage.

If those words sound familiar it's because I incorporated them in the poem I quoted in Chapter 7, 'Like Dew, Dancing'.

But if the Scottish Office was blighting in its reply, we were soon flooded with visitors, phone calls, letters, cards, as friends learnt about my cancer. I was so overwhelmed I decided to keep an album, but you can't mount phone calls, nor special healing oil from Russia, nor hot egg flans. So, you won't be surprised to learn, I wrote a poem.

Benefits

You cannot tabulate kindness,
    visits from friends,
letters and flowers,
    prayers and hot flans
which Helen brings wrapped in bright foil;
nor Svetlana's sea buckthorn oil;
nor laughter and poems;
nor the mellow sun ray
which day after day
    rinses old stonework.

For these there's no meagre benefit book,
    doled-out allowance.

But uncalculated abundance –
    a generous fabric
    which holds life in place.

Touched and uplifted, I still struggled to deal with my
daughter's illness. One of the collects in the Anglican
Prayer Book seemed particularly appropriate for me and
Elaine: 'Almighty God, you see that we have no power in
ourselves to help ourselves. Keep us both outwardly in
our bodies and inwardly in our minds that we may be
defended from all adversities which may afflict the body
and all evil thoughts which assault and hurt the soul.'

'Outwardly in our bodies', 'inwardly in our minds' . . .
I've got cancer, she's got schizophrenia – body and mind
are both under 'assault'. We cannot be defended *from* the
ills of the body, which is mortal and will die, but we can
be defended *in* them and even, I pray, *within* the 'evil
thoughts' which assault the person who suffers from
persecutory delusions and darkness.

I gathered these thoughts into a poem for my daughter,

reflecting on the meaning of our names, seeking for healing which never comes.

My name means sea-water,
    foaming white.
I would wash you, my daughter,
    whose name means 'bright';
would purge from you forever
    delusions and fear,
be your white witch to charm
    your hurt, your harm;
weave words of delight about your hair;
    undo all the darkness,
    release you,
    young as you were;
restore you your motherhood, your own baby dear.

But words have no potency
    well-springs no flow;
love has no meaning
in the non-life where you go.
Only hard needles, a mask
to dampen despair. Therefore I ask
forlornly for healing – heavens are brass,
good words mere mockery
and your sweet youth has passed
into the shadows,
    while others go free;
and you are stranded –
    without recovery.

'Words have no potency' and all I could do was listen while
Elaine poured out her bewilderment that her daughter
had never been returned to her. 'Why did the Social
Worker remove me from my home? Couldn't she have

helped me in my home and let us be as we were, instead of all this heart-wrenching experience and suffering due to the fact that I'm separated from my daughter and from my role as her mother. That's what's so painful and ever since then my life's been very difficult and full of misery.'

She attended her first children's panel with her brother to support her. Her husband, predictably, didn't turn up and decisions were deferred. Elaine said so often during those months of autumn 1995, 'I've never forgiven anyone for putting me into hospital and taking Margaret away. The pain, the absolute wrench . . .'. I always felt my heart twist as she talked. 'I take her to see you as often as I can,' I would say, 'and when I'm ill after my chemos, Paul and Carol bring her here whenever they can for you to come and see her.'

'I know, but it's not the same. It won't be right until I have her here under my roof.'

And what was there to say in reply? Nothing at all, but once a friend called on me while Margaret and Elaine were with me for the day. His name is Martyn and he's a journalist and a very fine poet. When the time came to take Margaret back across the city to Carol, having had her with us all day, Martyn kindly offered to take us by taxi – a major detour for him. We dropped Elaine off. 'This is where I part with my baby again', she said and made her lonely way to the lift and home.

Martyn told me about his father. He's 91 and he has always been a voracious reader, but now, limited and frail, he gets bad headaches when he reads. Martyn went on, 'In prayer I ask if he could stop having headaches and enjoy his books again. But the headaches continue. Healing,' Martyn concluded, 'is something deeper than cure.'

Until research can come up with an understanding of the causes of schizophrenia, a cure is as far away as ever.

And I, and six million other mothers like me in Britain alone, continue to walk our pilgrim way without sign-posts. But, in the love which surrounds me, I know I'm not alone. God may seem silent, but people are not. Their love surrounds Elaine, too. I tell her, 'People all over the world, people you don't even know, pray for you every day.' They stand in front of icons or light small candles, they pray in groups or alone. They write letters and phone. When they pray it is in the languages of Africa; they pray in Singhalese, too, in Portuguese, in Spanish, Russian, Polish, German, in tongues known and unknown, for Elaine and for her little Margaret, encircled by her godfamily, her grandparents, her own 'blood' Mum. This is the 'generous fabric which holds life in place'.

CHAPTER 10

An Extended Family

Among the mail which came flooding as friends heard about my cancer was an icon-style card painted in Wales. It shows a woman on her knees, her hands upraised in prayer. A startled hare runs to her for shelter. The card had come from our brothers John and Roland in their wooden huts. 'You are that little hare', John said and he unfolded the story of St Melangell, an Irish princess who left her homeland on that ageless journeying, the pilgrim's quest. In the green valleys of Wales, Melangell found shelter and a place to pray, but one day her seclusion was disturbed by the royal hunt. A startled hare ran out of the thicket and raced towards Melangell who scooped it up into her arms. At that moment the hunt came close. Melangell was probably as much at risk from the huntsmen as the trembling hare was, but a miracle happened. The huntsman's horn froze to his lips and no sound came forth. The hounds stopped snarling in their tracks. The prince rode up and seeing how securely the hare nestled in Melangell's arms, he promised her his protection. He gave her the field in which she prayed and a shrine was built there. To this day no one kills hares in St Melangell's valley. Her shrine has been rebuilt and is now a centre of prayer for healing, particularly for those who suffer from cancer.

As our house-hunting continued, seemingly fruitlessly,

I said to the Lord, 'You gave Melangell a field, surely a small house isn't too much of a problem?'

It was an anxious winter. Despite being on Section, Elaine slipped off medication and we watched her go down. Her Community Psychiatric Nurse was off sick. She faced three children's panels and we were still homeless. Stuart had no time for house-hunting and I had no energy. Chemotherapy was followed by radiotherapy – less drastic, but bringing a build-up of tiredness. One frosty January evening, as I waited for a machine to be free, knowing that Elaine was about to attend her third children's panel, thankful that her brother had agreed to go with her, I wrote the following poem.

Awaiting Radiotherapy

Awash with sub-zero sunset
the Castle is translucent – seems to float
above its crag,
a watercolour, which dulls
as the sun dips.
And I, blistered with radium
watch the last gold rays etch
the contours of a naked birch.

Look up. The lone bastion
is floodlit now against encroaching night.

I marvel at the potency of light.

The day of the children's panel I had a day off treatment – the machines need to be repaired regularly. I lay in bed, thankful for stillness and rest. The phone shrilled. It was a doctor from the casualty ward. 'Your daughter has been brought in by the police. She thought her coffee was poisoned and went to the police, taking the cup with her. They brought her to us. We've checked with the psychiatrist and he thinks it's an attack of stress. Can you collect her? We could put her in a taxi, but she has no money.'

I put down the receiver, wearily, and phoned Elaine's brother. 'When I'm in my coffin, someone will knock on the lid and tell me Elaine needs to be collected.'

So, I attended the panel with Elaine after all. We sat in the small waiting room, its bare walls covered with graffiti. I remembered similar waits with disturbed young people in police cells in social work days long ago and it saddened me to think that my gentle daughter was going through all this. We had a very long wait in these comfortless surroundings, but, against all expectations, Gary turned up.

His co-operation impressed the panel and so did the presentation which Elaine had prerecorded for them. They were not in the least forbidding and listened with respect and interest to Elaine's tape. Here is what she said.

Firstly, I'd like to say that Margaret was never taken from me on grounds that I wasn't able to look after her, but merely because the doctors had declared a situation to be one where they thought that I would be better off in hospital. So obviously I had to comply and it was heart-rending to know that the family was being broken up. We thought that this would only go on for a few months and that, by the time I came back, Margaret would be returned to me, but the whole process has been dragged out for a long, long time and everybody's had to change and adapt around it and we feel that it's about time that somebody does something about it, something in our favour because the basic fact is that we are a family, we want to be together and there's no way that anybody's going to tell us anything different. The Social Worker however, suggested that, in some cases, children are put up for adoption, but in my case I feel that this is totally unnecessary; it's never been a question for anybody because Margaret was God's gift to me and I've never done anything to dispute that or jeopardize that at all. And I think that if anybody even suggests this to me, then this would be totally out of the question.

Gary and I have gone through an awful lot in these months, realizing that the decision is all in the hands of the panel. That wasn't easy to accept, but we feel that this time it will go for us and that we will be able to say at the end of the day that Margaret is coming back to us as a family and that she will be within our care and nurture and everything will be back to normal again. We feel that so many forces have been against us during this time that it wouldn't be fair to say that Margaret wasn't to come back to us because we just couldn't accept that fact. It would be just too devastating for us. This maybe would give you a warning as to how we actually feel about it. We feel so strongly that Margaret should be ours that we're not prepared to accept any other fact.

I appreciate the role of the social workers and the panel, but also they have failed to recognize my potential or my capabilities in being a person and being a mother. I feel this is one of the facts you should be considering when you're about to decide what's what.

Gary added, sadly, 'I feel I've lost my kid.'

The panel gave Elaine and Gary a chance to prove themselves as parents by attending weekly sessions with Margaret at a children's centre for the next four months.

Elaine attended twice a week, almost without exception. Once again, she sat under observation in a room with her daughter. Gary was asked to come once a week, but it was all too much for him and he didn't come at all.

During that winter, I read a book in which a character debates whether God is all-love or all-powerful, for the evidence shows that he cannot be both. As I thought it through, I agreed and I settled for a God who is all-love.

Yet is God who is not all-powerful God?

Bit by bit, through the debilitating effects of chemotherapy, the awfulness and hopelessness of schizophrenia, I came to see that the love of God is the power of God. And the power of God is the love of God. There is nothing else.

I recalled words spoken by one of the mystics, a woman called Angela, who exulted, 'Behold the plenitude of God.' But then God said, 'Behold now and see my humility'.

And so we see Jesus. In the desert, fasting, tempted by Satan, Jesus refused to act against the laws of nature and turn stones to bread. But as he rode into Jerusalem he declared that the very stones over which he travelled would shout for joy. He knew this because he was riding to his death. He was about to tread the pathway of pain.

It's very hard to face pain and it's right not to underestimate it. Pain is appalling. It puts each sufferer into a private box. The rest of us stand outside. We can guess at but never feel, another's pain. Pain is entirely individual and yet it is universal, too. Pain is a universal language spoken by those who have no other voice.

There is no beauty in pain and there can be no truth, for pain mars what was lovely and distorts what was true. So, there seems to be no God. The level of separation is too great. God is good. How can a good God send pain? Pain alienates. How then can there be pain in God? If there is pain in God, why should I seek God at all? I desire beauty, colour, warmth, comfort, not the harsh contours of pain.

Seeking an answer, if we turn towards Jesus, in the midst of his triumph we find him in tears. Once again, I recall the blessing of sorrow which I carry on my journey.

In the end, however, we came upon a house. It was none of our planning, it just worked out – and it's less than a mile from where our granddaughter lives with Carol and Paul. All the joy our house brings was summed up in Palm Sunday Poem for Margaret, the third poem for my granddaughter from the pen of George Mackay Brown. It includes the words, 'Your feet are among the first daisies' and, indeed, Margaret's first toddling steps were deep in daisies across our garden, but I couldn't write and tell George, nor even thank him for his lovely poem. 'We all go through the green gate into April', he wrote. He died on the eve of Easter.

Margaret continued to run, laughing, among long grass and daisies. Our house is just right for her, and right for us all because our aim, with Carol and Paul, is to form an extended family around Elaine and Margaret. The process is underway for Carol and Paul to adopt their goddaughter. Long ago, godfamilies were called godsibs. This beautiful word has degenerated into the word 'gossip', but it was once a relationship which was held in great honour.

We see it reflected in the pen-pictures in Luke's Gospel of Mary's kinswoman, Elizabeth, of Joseph, Simeon, Anna. Like the Russian *staretz*, these are hidden people, and perhaps none more so than Elizabeth in those last months of her late and unexpected pregnancy. We may imagine her at home, wearily pushing back the weight of her greying hair, and turning her heavy body as light footsteps run to her curtained threshold and a young girl's voice calls her name. Elizabeth responds with a cry of joy.

Secluded, more than a little afraid of the birth to come, Elizabeth must have felt in need of comfort, too. Now God visits her in the tenderest, most acceptable way possible: through Mary. If the young girl needed Elizabeth's counsel and advice, the older woman needed Mary's companionship and trust. She encourages Mary's faith. There is no place for criticism, curiosity, condemnation. Elizabeth totally accepts Mary and her unborn child.

It takes great generosity to perceive the hidden potential in one another! Elizabeth offers her young kinswoman full and free hospitality, a place where both women can share their delight in Mary's motherhood.

The support Carol has given Elaine has meant being knocked up at midnight by the police, when Elaine has run away from hospital. It means continuing to hold on when the person she used to know often seems locked in a shell. Above all, it has meant taking on all the responsibility and care of a child, but also – and this is what is so unique and amazing – Carol continues to give Elaine access to her daughter and reassures her that 'Mummy' describes the person closest to you: Carol is 'Mum'.

Last autumn, when she was six, Susan (my youngest godgranddaughter!) told me about the video she was watching. Then she added, 'I know another story. It's in the Bible and it's true.' She told me about Moses. 'His mummy couldn't look after him so the princess took him home. That's like us and Margaret.'

For their part, despite their hurt, their anger and incomprehension, Gary and Elaine have obeyed all the rules about access to their baby. The pain of parting from Margaret is very real, but Elaine has conducted herself valiantly and with quiet dignity and, in honour of her I wrote the following poem.

Snowdrops

She grew slender as a snowdrop;
loved defenceless things:
seals, and the tremulous pearl
the last ebb of summer light
leaves where waves have been . . .

at length budded forth
her own small sunflower
– dear sundered heart.

Each spring in city gardens
snowdrops defy the winds of winter;
light lean Lenten flames
along the route
which joins and parts
my daughter and the child she loves.

These storm-tossed flowers
are not more brave and gentle
than a young mother
required to relinquish
the child she has borne.

The final children's panel was held on a balmy autumn day. Once again, Elaine attended without her husband, but with her brother's support. When it was over, he brought her up to us, to overnight – we didn't want her to be left on her own. She said very little, but looked across at me. 'So, Carol's going to adopt her', she said. Her eyes were full of pain.

She went upstairs to bed. Stuart and I went out to the garden to enjoy half an hour in the mellow sun. We had all thought perhaps it was better for Margaret not to come round on that particular day, but, to our joy, we saw her little fair head shining on Carol's shoulder. Carol showed us her gift for Elaine: a collage of family photographs with a Celtic blessing in the centre. On the back she had written: 'Dear Elaine, you haven't lost a daughter, but gained an extended family – forever.'

She went into the house with Margaret and we found that Elaine had tried to overdose on cough mixture and had made herself very sick, so the grandparents got busy, cleaning up, while Margaret and Carol paid a brief visit to Elaine.

Then, as if we weren't all traumatized enough, on her return home on the back of Carol's bike, Margaret's long leg swung into the spokes of the bike wheel and she broke a bone so small that it didn't show on the X-ray. Carol had to rush to hospital with Margaret. The bone mended quickly, but it was a horrible happening after Carol's gesture of love to ourselves and Elaine.

So that is the commitment we now share – to be an extended family in which Margaret meets her mother in the most natural, informal ways while she herself is totally secure in her relationship with Carol as her 'Mum'. Elaine continues to be supported by her Community Psychiatric Nurse, but her life has also been enriched by the input of her Home Help, Nancy, who radiates love and cheerfulness in the most natural way possible. We are also exploring the possibility of having a support worker in her home – who would be provided by Penumbra, but this involves a social worker's assessment.

Within that framework, Stuart and I must work out our continuing commitment to Russia. He's in St Petersburg as I write. I've booked tickets for my return. We are required to be equipped and all I see myself being is stripped.

Yet, as we equip ourselves for Russia – toothpaste, vitamin pills, medicines for friends, winter boots, you name it, we take it – we are aware that, as one writer has put it, however much you bring in, 'all Western things turn to stone as soon as they pass the frontier'. And I reflect that the pain of the cross, the darkness, must also be part of the resources God wants to fill us with. My friend who told me that the *staretz* had blessed me with sorrow, that sorrow is a blessing, for 'our sorrows shelter us in the wounds of Christ' also said, 'How can you and Stuart go to the people of Russia without the blessing of sorrow?'

Russia has borne the cross so long – as well as the blasphemy of atheism. A nineteenth-century poet wrote, 'The haughty eye of the foreigner fails to perceive the thing which shines across your humble nakedness, my native land: for in the guise of a slave, bowed with the weight of the cross, the King of Heaven has walked the length and breadth of you, blessing you.'

'Blessing you', yes, with sorrow.

To end this book, I asked Elaine to write down some thoughts about how life is for her now. Not surprisingly after all she's gone through, she's not so well, we feel, and that is reflected in what she writes.

Slowly my faith disappears as I feel more and more consumed by the world. My husband seems convinced that there is no God and punishes me for the times when I'm being me and when I believe. As I came back from hospital, I felt people were insulting me, giving me the stigma of a mental patient and basically trying to take away from what I intrinsically was. In these latter days there have been 'wars and rumours of war' and my mind sometimes seems unable to cope with difficulties that confront me. I need to feel safe and secure and sure of my world – and this isn't always the case. I feel trapped and insecure. I feel happy and contented when I'm with my baby. She's the sweetest thing that God ever blessed me with. She drains my energy sometimes, but we share some wonderful moments. My childhood was such that sometimes only the memories of it keep me going, but this gets to me, too: I feel I haven't lived up to my childhood.

In my diary I have sketched a figure of Elaine with Margaret in her upraised arms and underneath I've written the words of Jesus, 'Woman, be free.' I continue to pray for Elaine to be free, but I realized then that those words are directed at me. 'Woman, be free!' I replied, 'I can't be free, because she is not free, but the words are still there: 'Woman, be free'. The poems I have written in this book are part of my quest for freedom, to be like the dew, dancing. And so here is the last poem.

Be

Be content
with space and silence,
a lesser flight

for a girl, grounded.
Be glad
of conversation, the grace

of being. Together –
and no word said.

Yes, and the late light of midsummer
washes the peaceful harbour:
balm for troubled soul.

Rejoice:
she is your daughter.

But, oh, if her child lay folded
once again against her shoulder
and she were whole . . .

we would remember
loss no longer;
unlock larksong, laughter,

stretch forth untrammelled hands:

be.

The Society for Promoting Christian Knowledge (SPCK) has as its purpose three main tasks:

- **Communicating the Christian faith in its rich diversity**
- **Helping people to understand the Christian faith and to develop their personal faith**
- **Equipping Christians for mission and ministry**

SPCK Worldwide serves the Church through Christian literature and communication projects in over 100 countries. Special schemes also provide books for those training for ministry in many parts of the developing world. SPCK Worldwide's ministry involves Churches of many traditions. This worldwide service depends upon the generosity of others and all gifts are spent wholly on ministry programmes, without deductions.

SPCK Bookshops support the life of the Christian community by making available a full range of Christian literature and other resources, and by providing support to bookstalls and book agents throughout the UK. SPCK Bookshops' mail order department meets the needs of overseas customers and those unable to have access to local bookshops.

SPCK Publishing produces Christian books and resources, covering a wide range of inspirational, pastoral, practical and academic subjects. Authors are drawn from many different Christian traditions, and publications aim to meet the needs of a wide variety of readers in the UK and throughout the world.

The Society does not necessarily endorse the individual views contained in its publications, but hopes they stimulate readers to think about and further develop their Christian faith.

For further information about the Society, please write to:

SPCK, Holy Trinity Church, Marylebone Road,
London NW1 4DU, United Kingdom.
Telephone: 0171 387 5282